Good Little Ship

Arthur Ransome on board *Nancy Blackett*

GOOD LITTLE SHIP

Arthur Ransome, Nancy Blackett and the Goblin

PETER WILLIS

Lodestar Books

Published 2017 by
Lodestar Books
71 Boveney Road, London, SE23 3NL, United Kingdom

www.lodestarbooks.com

Copyright © Peter Willis 2017
The right of Peter Willis to be identified as the author
of this work has been asserted by him in accordance with the
Copyright, Designs and Patents Act 1988

A CIP catalogue record for this book
is available from the British Library

ISBN 978-1-907206-42-9

Typeset by Lodestar Books in Equity

Printed in Spain by Graphy Cems, Navarra

All papers used by Lodestar Books
are sourced responsibly

MIX
Paper from
responsible sources
FSC® C007507
FSC
www.fsc.org

Contents

List of Illustrations

List of Plates

(between pages 112 and 113)

To Wendy, Eleanor and Paula
with thanks for their support
and forbearance in accepting
Nancy as an adopted daughter
in the family

Foreword

by Libby Purves

W*e Didn't Mean to Go to Sea* was for me, and countless others, the spark of a love affair. As a child I was given other Arthur Ransome books, and mildly enjoyed the Swallows' and Amazons' adventures in the Lakes, and the muddy world of *Secret Water*. Later, already having sailed the Atlantic myself as a yacht crew and fallen in love with the tall-ships races, I quite enjoyed the treasure-hunting of *Peter Duck* and the fantasy of *Missee Lee*.

But *We Didn't Mean to Go to Sea* is different: neither children's play on calm waters in reach of rescue, nor a piratical fantasy either. It stands alone because every stage of the *Goblin*'s accidental voyage to Vlissingen is deliberate, possible, thrillingly solid. It could happen. Every danger on the way is real and familiar to anyone who sails our British waters in a small boat: seasickness, sandbanks, rising wind necessitating a grit-teethed, panicky reefing operation. There are big ships, worries about navigation lights, and that uncertainty, so familiar before the days of GPS, as to where you actually are when dawn breaks.

John's anxiety about salvage and grounding is rational, not a child's bogeyman fears. The responsibility he takes for his siblings, and their various fear, trust and gallantry, make reading it at times intensely moving. When, rushing through the dark at the helm of the little *Goblin*, the eldest looks below to see her sleeping crew, what fills him is universal—a sense that every lone night-watch keeper in dark waters can feel with him: 'a serious kind of joy'. Who, among small-boat offshore sailors, does not remember the night when 'for the first time crew and ship were in his charge, his alone'? And the serious joy of it?

I read the book when I had just started sailing, finding myself—after putting a small-ad in *Yachting Monthly*—at the bidding of a random set of skippers, longing to learn, enamoured of every sail and sheet, entranced by the timeless practicalities of rope and canvas. At work, as a young *Today* presenter, I would fill in the duller moments during 'Thought for the Day' doodling layouts of possible boats on the edge of the script. The *Goblin* was always the matrix, the basis of any ideal boat: her origin, as this engrossing book celebrates, was dear *Nancy Blackett*, which still sails our East coast waters.

When, with my then boyfriend (now husband) we bought our first boat it was a 26ft Contessa: modern in comparison to *Goblin* but with the same long keel and squared stern, the graceful hull and simple tiller that we instinctively trusted. We polished our brass lamps, cherished the woodwork of the little cabin, and felt the way the children do in the book: trusting a good little ship. We knew that while we were amateurs the boat was a professional, her design refined over generations to take the seas with grace.

Later came other boats, bigger ones, but always we eschewed the modern wide, caravan-like, light-finned yachts and the sleek racers in favour of solidity, the narrow sobriety of handholds, heavy keels and a shape made gracious by centuries of knowledge. Thus *Goblin* and *Nancy Blackett* helped to shape our sailing. And for me at least, on many a night passage with an unwelcome forecast, the spirit of the book was a kind of comfort. I have looked down into a lamplit cabin and seen my children sleeping, and my husband rolled up off-watch in a blanket but with boots still on, and let them all sleep longer. That serious joy means looking forward to raising the first shorelights alone and waking them to the good news, as pleased as if you've lit them yourself. It is a joy born of responsibility, of competence, of rejoicing in the boat herself, as she cuts through the waves and leans to the slope of the wind.

Adrian Seligman wrote of far bigger ships, the old square-riggers on the great grain race, 'a sailing ship at sea is one of God's most patient, yet most steadfast and courageous creatures'. A little yacht, a humble yacht like *Goblin*, has its share of that glory. And, as Seligman adds, 'those who live with her, who watch her day by day... these people learn from her, in time'. We all have.

Libby Purves
August 2017

Preface

There's more than a touch of irony about the title of Arthur Ransome's *We Didn't Mean to Go to Sea*. The book came about precisely because that's just what he had intended to do. He and Evgenia had moved house from the inland waters of the Lake District to the East Coast—and simultaneously sought out and bought a sea-going cruising yacht—with the express intention of rediscovering coastal and offshore sailing, something they'd last done, to any serious extent, with *Racundra*, in the Baltic, over ten years previously.

The boat was, of course, the *Nancy Blackett*. The house they found was a former farmhouse at Levington on the north bank of the River Orwell in Suffolk, overlooking Harwich Harbour. But their real home quickly came to be Pin Mill, where *Nancy Blackett*'s mooring lay. Ransome loved its convivial atmosphere, the cheerful comings and goings of fellow boatowners and their families in the season, the Butt and Oyster pub by the waterside and the real Miss Powell's tearoom next door.

No wonder that he set the opening of *We Didn't Mean to Go to Sea* here—'down the deep green lane that ended in the river itself... this happy place where almost everyone wore sea-boots and land, in comparison with water, seemed hardly to matter at all.'—and also of the book that followed it, *Secret Water*.

This sense of community, and the liberation of being able to sail a proper yacht in tidal waters, had a tonic effect on his writing. 'I was really afraid I'd done for myself or rather for these stories by uprooting,' he wrote to his editor at Jonathan Cape, 'but I haven't. This new idea is the best since *Swallows and Amazons*.'

It certainly was. *We Didn't Mean to Go to Sea* is of a different calibre from the rest of the books. In saying this I don't mean to denigrate them at all, but—as I hope to show in the succeeding pages—it sets out to do more, and succeeds. The plotting is tighter, and the theme, like the boat and the waters on which it sails, is bigger. It is a true 'rite of passage' tale. And Ransome put a lot more of himself into the book. Little wonder that when he had finished it, he felt a need to wind down with a more gentle adventure, exploiting the local East Coast landscape in *Secret Water*. And when he had done that, as we see in Chapter 5, he felt, albeit perhaps briefly, that his work, as far as these children were concerned, was done.

The Ransomes spent just five years in Suffolk. It might well have been a lot longer—after about four years at Levington they found Harkstead Hall, on the right side of the Orwell and about two miles inland from Pin Mill, and were very happy there for some 18 months. But the Second World War, with the heavy air raids over East Anglia, forced them to retreat to the Lake District. When the war was over, they thought about moving back, and even had another boat, *Peter Duck*, built by Harry King. But life moved on in different directions. They found a Thames-side flat in south London, and then discovered the south coast, around the Solent, and went to David Hillyard of Littlehampton, who had built *Nancy Blackett*, and ordered first one, and then another boat to be built there.

So the East Coast years were in the end a brief interlude, but an extremely happy, productive one, and this present book is, amongst other things, a celebration of it. It's also about the boat, the *Nancy Blackett*, in both her real life, or lives, and her fictional one; about the book that contained the latter, and about the author of that book.

I don't intend to include a potted biography of Arthur Ransome here; there are plenty of other books for that. At times his life was colourful, eventful and even dangerous—though he was quite good at enhancing that colour here and there. (I do wonder about the 'keepers of some performing bears' with whom he claims to have kept company in France—they crop up in his study of Robert Louis Stevenson, but not elsewhere.) Suffice to say that by the time he reached Suffolk, in his fifty-first year, he had been around enough to have had some corners knocked off, and acquired some depth and complexity. And to have learned how to wear it lightly.

Even the apparent simplicity of his writing in these books is complex. He worked and worked and worried about his books. He even submitted them to Genia for approval or criticism, which may or may not have been helpful (could that whole 'critic on the hearth' thing have been a sort of private joke between them?). He was a craftsman who had developed his craft. Compare the language in the early studies of Stevenson, or Oscar Wilde—abstruse, technical and sometimes well-nigh impenetrable—with that of *Old Peter's Russian Tales*: much simpler as you'd expect, but still fussy and rather ornate. It has a hangover of that authorial voice of the narrator attempting to create a path between the reader and the subject, which nowadays we think of as merely getting in the way. And then compare that with the language of the *Swallows and Amazons* books—plain, and direct. At least on first acquaintance—but it's cunningly loaded with all sorts of nuances, subtexts, points of view, attitudes to his characters and often quiet jokes. And this is what makes his books so easily readable and yet so satisfying.

My own exposure to Arthur Ransome began when I was about eleven. My mother was in the habit of bringing back half a dozen books—the maximum allowance—from the children's library whenever she went into town for her shopping, and this was the day they were due back. I'd read all the others, and the only one left was this thick green book, with the slightly odd illustrations. I can picture myself, lying on my stomach on the living-room floor, totally, at last, wrapped up in it, and begging her not to take it back. I can't recall whether she left it, or took it back to be renewed, but I do know I was hooked. This was *Swallowdale*, and I followed it up with all the others, in whatever order they came to hand.

It would have been twenty years later that I'd arranged to help a friend to sail his parents' yacht, a tubby plastic twenty-eight-foot Sea Rover class boat called *Tomina*, across to the Baltic ready for them to start their summer holidays. She was moored at Pin Mill, and for me, coming for the first time down that 'deep, green lane' to join her was a magical experience, rather like stepping into Narnia.

We spent many holidays and weekends over the next few years on the Orwell, and the other rivers, the Deben, the Ore, and on the Backwaters, sailing and exploring in a variety of boats, but it wasn't until 1993 that I renewed my acquaintance with Ransome's books. We bought my elder daughter *Swallows and Amazons*, in the early Red Fox paperback edition. It rekindled my affection for Ransome—and indeed we read the whole series aloud together, a chapter (or two or three) at bedtime, and eventually squeezing in another, or two, before school in the morning. But it also had a notice in the back about the Arthur Ransome Society, not long formed, and we joined. I, being an adult, and bookish, took it all very seriously, and acquired all the books on Ransome I could find: Christina Hardyment's *Arthur Ransome and Captain Flint's Trunk*, the Brogan biography, Peter Hunt's *Approaching Arthur Ransome*, and of course Roger Wardale's *Nancy Blackett*.

I think now I may have been a mid-life man in need of an obsession (and one who couldn't get enthusiastic about motorbikes), so this was it. I joined the society's southern regional committee (we were living in Surrey then), edited its newsletter, organized events—and traipsed up to Suffolk when I heard that *Nancy Blackett* was to take part in a race with another of Ransome's boats, *Peter Duck*. The rest, you might say, was simply inevitable. When *Nancy Blackett* came up for sale, a couple of years later, I had the idea that the Arthur Ransome Society might buy her. Perhaps I wasn't the only one to think that, but I decided to write to various likely members suggesting the idea, and forced it onto the agenda at the next AGM. In the end the Society decided—perhaps wisely I now have to admit—not to do that, but by then people were sending me money, and it seemed easier to go along with the belief that it could happen than to send all the money back.

And that is how, twenty years ago, the Nancy Blackett Trust was born. What would have become of *Nancy* if it hadn't been? Who knows? Perhaps some wealthy fan would have bought her (there was a rumour that Hergé, the Belgian creator of Tintin, was interested), or maybe she would have passed on through a succession of more—or less—devoted and capable private owners. But it would only have taken one to break the chain...

As it is, *Nancy* has settled into a useful life, as a floating ambassador for Arthur Ransome and his books, providing a taste of the sea-sailing he came to Suffolk to enjoy, and giving her many visitors a chance to experience the feeling of being aboard the *Goblin*. For me, running the Trust became at times like having a second job, one that came with great satisfaction. But it also had an effect on my main career, leading to jobs on the editorial teams of *Classic Boat*, and later *Classic Sailor,* magazines where I was privileged to sail aboard and write about many fine boats (including *Nancy* herself on occasion).

It also led, inevitably, to a deepening love for the Suffolk coast, which resulted, about three years ago, in Wendy and me moving to Woodbridge, where I can report we are very happily settled and where I can keep a closer eye on *Nancy* (no more slogging up the M25 and the A12), and get involved in planning further adventures for her.

This year, the twentieth anniversary of the Nancy Blackett Trust's formation, is by a happy coincidence the eightieth anniversary of *We Didn't Mean to Go to Sea*'s publication, marked by the local community on the Shotley peninsula, with much help from the Trust, in several ways, not least of which was the adoption of the name 'Arthur Ransome's East Coast'.

Peter Willis
Woodbridge
August 2017

'Good little ship': reportedly Ransome's favourite photo of *Nancy Blackett*

PART ONE

Ransome

CHAPTER ONE

Inspiration

℘

'**A** little white cutter with red sails was coming in towards the moored boats.'
For the four children, paddling about in a dinghy among the moorings, this sighting is the beginning of an encounter which will lead to them sailing this same boat—alone and unaided, through varied perils—across the North Sea to Holland.

The children are fictitious as, for the most part, is their adventure: this is the start of Arthur Ransome's *We Didn't Mean to Go to Sea*. But the location is real enough—Pin Mill on the River Orwell in Suffolk, where Ransome was living while he wrote the book. As for the 'little white cutter', she has a fictional name, but she was, and is, very real indeed. Ransome had not long previously sailed his own newly-acquired boat up that same river, and into those same moorings. He had named her the *Nancy Blackett*, but in *We Didn't Mean to Go to Sea*, she becomes the *Goblin*.

'Funny name for a boat,' comments Roger, the youngest of the children, who is reading the name on a vacant mooring buoy. 'I wonder where she is?'

They soon find out, for sure enough, the boat coming up the river is the *Goblin*, and she is being sailed single-handed.

> Someone was busy on her foredeck . As they watched, they saw the tall red mainsail crumple and fall in great folds on top of the cabin. 'There's no-one at the tiller', said John. 'I say,' said Roger. 'Is he all alone?'

Indeed he is, but he seems to know his boat well enough, as he prepares to sail onto his mooring, using the jib, watched by the children who pull their dinghy clear just in time.

He was standing up, steering with a foot on the tiller, with his eyes on the buoy ahead of him. Suddenly, when he was still a few yards from it, they saw him stoop and then run forward along the side deck. The jib was flapping. The young man had grabbed the boathook, and was waiting, ready to reach down and catch the buoy.

'He'll just do it,' Titty said, almost in a whisper.

'Beautifully,' said John.

'Oh,' gasped Titty. 'He can't reach it.'

For the boat has stopped moving a moment too soon. The boathook is an inch too short, then a foot. She is being swept back by the tide onto other moored boats. In desperation the skipper hurls a rope to the children in the dinghy; John makes it fast to the buoy in a swift, seamanlike manner, and they are thus, with a bowline knot, instantly bonded with the *Goblin* and her skipper.

These are the children originally encountered by readers of Arthur Ransome as the Swallows in *Swallows and Amazons*, the first of his children's novels, where they enjoy dinghy-sailing adventures in the Lake District. *Swallow*, sailed by the Walker children, Captain John, Mate Susan, Able-Seaman Titty and Ship's Boy Roger, and *Amazon*—of which the 'master and part-owner' is Nancy Blackett, with her sister Peggy 'mate and part-owner of the same'—were both based on real dinghies. Their lake is a fictional construct, but it combines elements of Coniston and Windermere, and individual locations are identifiable.

Ransome liked to set his stories in locations he knew and loved. After three more books (*Swallowdale*, *Winter Holiday* and *Pigeon Post*) set in the Lakes, where he then lived, and one (*Coot Club*) on the Norfolk Broads, where he'd occasionally hire a yacht, and where the locations in the book are entirely real, and not rearranged and disguised as in the Lakes books, plus one fantastical yarn (*Peter Duck*) set in the Caribbean (though starting prosaically enough from Lowestoft), he hankered after doing some sea-sailing and persuaded his wife Evgenia that they should move to the East Coast.

They discovered the Shotley peninsula, between the rivers Orwell and Stour, though in the end they rented a house at Levington, on the other side of the Orwell, just across, and down a bit, from Pin Mill.

At that time he was just finishing the proof-correcting and illustrations for *Pigeon Post*, his sixth book, and worrying that he was running out of ideas. He had no idea where his next plot was going to come from, but his main concern at that stage was to start the offshore sailing which had inspired the move, and that meant finding a boat.

The boat he eventually bought was to solve both these problems, as well as providing the role model for the *Goblin*. She was a Hillyard 7-tonner, 28ft 6in long, about five years old, lying in Poole Harbour and at that stage named *Electron*. Ransome bought her on the spot and promptly rechristened her *Nancy Blackett* after his favourite character—'but for Nancy, I would never have been able to buy her,' he said.

A young crewman, Peter Tisbury, was engaged, 'strong enough to do the heavy work of pulling and hauling, and young enough not to want to take a share in the navigation to which, after 10 years away from the sea, I was most eagerly looking forward,'—and they set about sailing her back to the Orwell.

The delivery voyage, which immediately ran into a full gale, proved a great deal more eventful and exciting than someone who had done no offshore sailing for a decade or more might have wished.

'We started out from Poole on Sept 14, just as the famous gale began,' he wrote in a letter. 'We got to Yarmouth, Isle of Wight, where we learnt that the lifeboat had been warned to be ready by the coastguards at the Needles who had observed our approach... Sunday we lay quiet in Yarmouth. Monday we bussed into Cowes to get a storm jib made as we had none. That night... came the climax of the gale, of which you no doubt read in the newspapers. In Yarmouth two boats were flung on the breakwater, seven or eight sunk, one man was drowned and the lifeboat was out three times during the night *inside the harbour*. We spent the whole night fighting off a huge motor cruiser which had moored alongside us... Poor *Nancy* survived, bruised a great deal but not seriously damaged...'

In an alternative version of the tale, from a draft of the unpublished later part of his autobiography, he wrote: 'In some ways I could hardly have chosen a worse, and in others, I could hardly have chosen a better introduction to sailing on the coasts of England... I nearly lost the boat on the first day, mistakenly meeting all the force of the ebb out by the Needles and, in the wild weather, as nearly as possible being swept on the Shingles. However, we evaded them, found our way through by Hurst Castle and came to Yarmouth... I knew by that time that I had got a very good boat.'

Or as he put it in his log: 'Consider the boat pretty good and the engine a real beauty. But I must say I hope the next passage will be more like 'yachting'.'

After popping up to London for a couple of days to sign the lease on his new home at Broke Farm in Levington Ransome returned, had the dinghy repaired (for 5 shillings) and moved *Nancy* to Haslar Creek in Portsmouth Harbour, where his cousin Godfrey Ransome, who was in the Navy, visited the new boat.

They sailed again on the 23rd, pausing at Newhaven for a nap, then on again... 'cleared Beachy Head, passed by the Royal Sovereign Light Vessel and were presently going like a train past Dungeness, reaching Dover at 10 minutes past two in the afternoon, very wet and very cold and glad to get hot baths and a real dinner at the *Lord Warden*. Again the gales blew up...'

After a day in Dover they left for Ramsgate, 'with a promise, not kept, of easy weather'. They decided to skip Ramsgate and carried on, under trysail and in rain and wind. The boat's electrics failed, and Ransome describes them as 'Bucketing along in the dark, and able to see the compass only by occasional flashes of the torch.'

In his letter to the Gnosspelius family, dated 1 October, c/o the Butt and Oyster, Pin Mill, Ipswich, he also mentions, how, on 'that last wild night... the miserable navigation lights... blew out always the moment we showed them. I used a red Woolworth bakelite plate with a strong torch behind it, to frighten off the Flushing Harwich steamer !!!' He sums up: 'So here she is, and after ten years with none, I've had a little 'yachting'. It made me feel horribly old but in a way very young and inexperienced.'

In those last few words we can sense the seeds of the theme of *We Didn't Mean to Go to Sea* already forming in his mind. For Ransome, possibly to his surprise (he remarks, 'It's much more difficult than Baltic cruising'), sailing in tidal waters was a new level of experience, as it was to be for the young crew of the *Goblin*. His last big-boat sailing. as distinct from the dinghies of the Lake District, had been a good ten years previously, in his own *Racundra*, on the virtually tideless Baltic.

Night encounter

The whole experience: the wild night, the sheer shock of being solely responsible for something new and unfamiliar which is threatening to get out of control, even the Woolworth plate incident, seems to have poured itself into the plot of *We Didn't Mean to Go to Sea*. It is a book about mastering elemental forces, about using lessons learnt, knowledge gained and skills acquired to cope with an extreme situation involving real danger. It is about being tested, and triumphing. For the young Swallows, it is about moving from the comparatively safe confines of their beloved lake to the real world of tidal oceans, lee shores, large, threatening ships and the uncertainties of entering a foreign port. In short, it's about growing up.

The adventure starts uneventfully enough, with the Walker children, John, now aged about 14, Susan, 13, Titty, 11 and Roger, 9, newly-arrived in Pin Mill. With their mother, and much younger sister Bridget, they are staying at Alma Cottage and awaiting the arrival of their father, a naval officer, who is returning any day from an overseas posting to take up one at the nearby Shotley naval base.

After helping to tie up the *Goblin*, they are soon aboard, making themselves useful and chatting to her young skipper, Jim Brading. At 18 and just about to go up to University, he is a tantalising bit older than the elder Swallows. He is also very confident and knowledgeable about handling the boat—which belongs to his uncle, and which he has just sailed round from Dover—although perhaps he is not quite as wise as he thinks he is.

A friendship is quickly forged as the children help tidy the boat up.

'What's the furthest you've ever been in her?' asked John.

'Uncle Bob and I took her down to Falmouth and back one year.'

'We used to sail there with Daddy when he was on leave,' said John, 'but only in an open boat. We never had one we could sleep in.'

'Like to spend a night in the *Goblin*?' said Jim, smiling.

The new friendship is consolidated when they persuade Mother to invite him back to dinner, and he falls asleep over his soup. An invitation follows for a few days' sailing aboard the *Goblin*—just within the Orwell and Stour and Harwich Harbour, and back in time to meet their father off the continental ferry at Harwich. After some deliberation, plus a few local enquiries into Jim's capabilities and character, Mother agrees to let them go, subject to a few conditions: 'No night sailing, and no going outside the Harbour.'

They set off down river, with Jim imparting some of the rudiments of seamanship, chiefly to John, as they go. They spend the night anchored off Shotley and in the morning, after taking a look at the Beach End buoy, which defines the edge of the harbour and the beginning of the open sea, turn on the engine—there's no wind—with a view to motoring up to Ipswich.

They've not gone far, however, before the engine coughs and dies; out of petrol. They drop the anchor opposite Felixstowe, and Jim decides to row ashore and buy some, while Susan prepares breakfast.

Six hours later, he still hasn't come back. (He's been hit by a bus, but neither the Swallows nor the readers know that.) Fog has come down and the tide has risen. *Goblin* is dragging her anchor—John realises he should have paid out more chain. In trying to do so, he loosens it from the winch, and the entire chain, followed by a bit of frayed rope, by which it had been secured to the boat, flies overboard. John attempts to re-anchor using the kedge, but fails to stock it properly, so it too drags and they begin to drift with the tide. The first they know of this is when a buoy appears to be approaching them in the fog. It's the Beach End, and as they drift past it they realise they are out at sea. Exactly where they promised they wouldn't go.

Moreover, the *Goblin* is drifting, engineless, anchorless (too deep now for any available warp on the kedge) and without navigation lights—they ran out of paraffin on Jim's overnight trip from Dover. The wind is getting up.

John decides the only thing to do is get some sail on her. Susan is for sailing back to harbour, to try and repair their promise to Mother, but John persuades her of the dangers of shoals and an unknown lee shore in the fog. 'Get out to sea and stay there,' is the advice he remembers from Jim, and despite Susan's anxieties, compounded by seasickness, he is determined to follow it.

He navigates *Goblin* outside the shoals around the Cork Sand, and sets a course south-east by east. The wind, still from the south-west, increases in strength. At one point, when the fog lifts, they attempt to turn back, but the motion of the boat, sailing against the wind, is so awful that Susan quickly agrees to go on before the wind until it abates. John decides to take in a reef, nearly falls overboard just as he's done it, but is held by his lifeline. With this crisis past, and the handling of the boat eased, confidence returns to the crew. Susan's sea-sickness is cured and, as Titty expresses it, 'The ship was suddenly full of happiness'.

At one point they meet the night ferry from Flushing to Harwich, and are in danger of being run down by it until they remember Jim showing them how strong the torch was by shining it through one of the red Woolworth's bakelite plates (just as Ransome himself had) and commenting 'Good as a port light'.

Soon after dawn, in one of the few incidents Ransome didn't encounter on his delivery sail from Poole, they espy a kitten clinging to an empty chicken-coop, evidently washed off the deck of a cargo steamer, and manage to rescue it, christening it Sinbad.

By this time, John is beginning to consider the idea of carrying on, rather than turning back, though none of them knows what country, or what port, they are approaching. They see a pilot ship anchored offshore, and decide the right thing to do is to take a pilot on board.

But the decision to take a pilot raises another dilemma. What would he do if he discovered there were only four children and no grown-up aboard? Fears of being seized for salvage prey on their minds. The solution they adopt is to leave John, acting the ship's boy, on the tiller while the rest of them hide in the cabin making 'grown-up noises'. These consist largely of stamping feet to penny-whistle tunes, but they succeed in convincing the amiable pilot that the captain is finding relaxation in a drink after a hard passage.

He answers one of their unspoken questions as soon as he comes aboard.

'Good day, mynheer,' said the pilot, reaching for the tiller, 'You want me to take you into Flushing?'

As they come into Flushing, they pass a ferry just preparing to sail for Harwich. John recognises his father leaning over the rail—and Daddy recognises John. But the ship is already beginning to cast-off. It's just too late. Or is it? John and the pilot decide to moor the *Goblin* between them, to surprise her supposed captain, and then the truth about the crew is revealed. The pilot is impressed—'I would not cross de Nord Sea mine self in so small a boat'—when a motorboat arrives, bearing Daddy himself. Explanations follow.

Daddy, whose chief contribution to the series of books hitherto has been the famous telegram that signals permission for the start of the *Swallows and Amazons* adventure, 'Better drowned than duffers if not duffers won't drown', appears to take their story in his stride, though one or two comments indicate his appreciation of the gravity of the situation. When John explains how he set his course to clear the shoals near the Cork lightship, Daddy comments, 'You were a bit lucky, but it wasn't a bad idea.' Again, a little later, when Titty remarks, 'Wasn't it lucky we kept going straight?' his response gives a great deal away:

> 'A lot of things were lucky,' said Daddy, and suddenly, while they were walking along, brought his hand down on John's shoulder and gave it a bit of a squeeze. 'You'll be a seaman yet, my son.'

For John this is the highest compliment imaginable, and he accepts it in an appropriate, for him, way:

> He found himself biting his lower lip pretty hard, and looking the other way.

Daddy organises a telegram to Mother (disguising its origin so she will be merely angry rather than anxious), takes them for a meal, with John falling asleep at the table just like Jim Brading, and sails them back in *Goblin*. They pick up Jim, who has been in hospital with concussion all the while, and sail back to Pin Mill, to begin explaining things to Mother.

Thus recounted the tale seems, if not impossible, at least improbable. But it is part of Ransome's skill as a storyteller to make the improbable seem inevitable. The *Goblin* is almost a leading character in the book—the sense of being aboard her is vividly captured, her motion in the water accurately described. Whatever its other qualities, and they are many, *We Didn't Mean to Go to Sea* is a hymn of praise to *Nancy Blackett*, and Ransome's delight in bringing her to the page is almost palpable:

If anybody could have seen his face in the faint glimmer from the compass window, he would have seen that there was a grin on it. John was alone in the dark with his ship, and everybody else was asleep. He, for that night, was the Master of the *Goblin*, and even the lurches of the cockpit beneath him as the *Goblin* rushed through the dark filled him with a serious kind of joy. He and the *Goblin* together. On and on. On and on. Years and years hence, when he was grown up, he would have a ship of his own and sail her out into wider seas than this. But he would always and always remember this night, when for the first time crew and ship were in his charge, his alone.

So… and back… So…and back… Lean and sway with this triumphant motion. Good little ship. Good little ship. He put a hand over the edge of the coaming and patted the damp deck in the darkness.

Arthur Ransome bought *Nancy Blackett* in September 1935. Within a few months she'd given him the idea for the new book. On 16 January 1936, two days before his fifty-second birthday, he wrote to his publisher, G. Wren Howard at Jonathan Cape:

> Spirits here are rising again at last. During the last four days, I have seen, grabbed, clutched and pinioned a really gorgeous idea for another book. Swallows only. No Nancy or Peggy or Captain Flint. But a GORGEOUS idea with a first class climax inevitable and handed out on a plate. Lovely new angle of technical approach and everything else I could wish. So I breathe again. I was really afraid I'd done for myself or rather for these stories by uprooting, but I haven't.

Far from it, as we shall see in succeeding chapters. But it is not just his own beloved and well-understood little ship which Ransome brings to this book. It is as if writing about the sea, rather than inland lakes and rivers, releases something within him that is dormant in those other books. *We Didn't Mean to Go to Sea* possesses a richness and depth which the other titles—excellent in their own ways as they are—simply don't attempt. As well as his own experience, both in sailing *Nancy* back from Poole and over to Flushing to research the voyage, and earlier in *Racundra*, he draws on his heroes from the world of maritime literature to season the narrative with a salty authenticity which not only consolidated his reputation as a children's author, but also re-established him as a writer on yachting and the sea—an area which he had largely neglected since the publication of *Racundra's First Cruise* in 1923.

His biographer Hugh Brogan sums up *We Didn't Mean to Go to Sea* as 'a book of which Conrad would have been proud.'

Like Conrad, like Melville and an elect handful of other authors, Ransome creates in this book a tale which captures and understands that ineffable bond between man and the sea, and that fascination with it which draws people into sailing—and which puts an ironic twist on the apologetic assertion contained in its title.

He was back at the tiller, leaning on it again. He took another look at the compass card under that dim yellow glow, wedged himself against the cockpit coaming with a foot against the opposite seat, looked up at the part of the sky that was full of stars, and a little ashamedly admitted to himself that he was happy.

CHAPTER TWO

Good Little Ship

છ્ર

What was this boat, then, which captured Ransome's heart and inspired his pen? *Nancy Blackett*, looked at now, presents a pleasingly old-fashioned, even classic appearance: a long, low, white-painted hull, its length accentuated by a sizeable bowsprit, surmounted by varnished brightwork on the cockpit coamings, cabin and forehatch. Brass portholes adorn the cabin sides, with two more on its forward face, and there is an additional porthole let into the hull on the port bow—it gives light to the heads compartment, and provides *Nancy* with a distinctive identifying mark, when viewed from that side. A surprisingly tall mast, and a long boom, which extends a little beyond her transom stern, give a stately elegance to her lines.

The shape of her hull not too surprisingly matches exactly John's description of his ideal yacht at the beginning of *We Didn't Mean to Go to Sea*. As the children are paddling about the Pin Mill moorings they discuss which yacht they'd like to have. Susan chooses a big white one, with a long counter, but John quickly dismisses it. 'I'd rather have one with a square stern, like a quay punt. Daddy says they're twice as good in a seaway.' There's what might be called an element of authorial pre-emptive post-hoc rationalisation at work here, for the little white cutter coming up the river as he speaks has just such a stern, a flat transom, slightly raked.

The reference to quay punts also has a slightly prophetic ring to it, since they are closely identified with Falmouth, which is shortly to come up in the conversation. Ships used to lie off in the Falmouth Roads, about to cross the Atlantic or just in from doing so, and the quay punts were designed to ferry supplies out to them. They were typically up to 30ft long, gaff-rigged (unlike *Nancy*) but her lines are indeed descended from them.

Below her waterline lies a long, deep keel. When she sails, she heels quickly to a fairly sharp, sporty angle, and then stays there, picking up speed and moving surprisingly fast for an old lady of her age and size.

Anyone stepping aboard will find themselves sharing the cockpit with a long, carved tiller, and a wealth of varnished timber, on the locker lids and high coamings. The cockpit is reassuringly deep, though not quite as deep as when she was built—it was converted to self-draining in the 1990s. Astern, on the short after-deck, a pair of varnished, scissor-like crutches will probably be supporting the boom, while looking forward, there on the aft bulkhead of the cabin, just beside the companionway, is the curious large porthole, bigger than a dinner-plate, which attracts Susan's attention soon after she and the other Swallows are signed-on as crew of the *Goblin*.

'I found a tin of brass polish when I was tidying the place where the lamps are,' said Susan. 'Do you think it would be all right if I had a go at that porthole.' She was looking at the porthole through which the steersman could see the compass, which was hung inside the cabin, over the sink.

Jim puffed out some smoke and looked at the porthole as if he was seeing it for the first time.

'It has gone a bit green,' he said. 'You simply can't keep them bright.'

Of all the brasswork on *Nancy*, which is regularly polished by visitors, particularly children (a big tin of Brasso and some rags are permanently stored in one of the cockpit lockers, ready to hand for just this purpose), this one is indeed the hardest to keep bright.

But let's not linger in the cockpit. A ship may announce herself with her external shape and her sail plan, which will please the eye and provide much information for the knowledgeable sailor, but her secret heart is below, in her cabin. It exerts a magnetic fascination and no-one ever feels they have been truly aboard a boat until they have visited this inner sanctum. Once the Swallows have reached the cockpit of the *Goblin*, after helping to tie her up, it doesn't take them long to discover it.

'I say, just look down,' said Titty.

They looked down into the cabin of the little ship, at blue mattresses on bunks on either side, at a little table with a chart tied down to it with string, at a roll of blankets in one of the bunks, at a foghorn in another, and at a heap of dirty plates and cups and spoons in a little white sink opposite the tiny galley, where a saucepan of water was simmering on one of the two burners of a little cooking stove.

And that, in general terms, is just what any present-day visitor will see. A two-burner stove to starboard, and a white enamel sink to port, just inside the companionway. It's all just as in Ransome's illustration, 'Cooking and Steering', in *We Didn't Mean to Go to Sea*.

Then come the four blue bunks, two in the main cabin, two in the forward cabin. Knowledgeable young visitors invariably know whose was which. John to starboard, Roger to port in the saloon, Susan to starboard, Titty to port in the fo'c'sle. Fans of the book tend to dive for the bunk of their favourite character, and it's usually Titty's that attracts the most visitors.

Like all good ships, and in conformity with the Merchant Shipping Act of 1894, *Nancy* has her tonnages inscribed into her main beam (the transverse timber supporting the deck which is closest to the mast).

Tonnage, as a convenient way of indicating a yacht's size, has fallen out of use in recent decades and is more or less meaningless to many modern sailors, but it was common currency when *Nancy* was built, and when Ransome sailed her.

When *Goblin* ties up in Flushing and the harbourmaster inspects her Ship's Papers, he asks John for her tonnage.

'4.86,' said John, who by this time knew by heart the figures carved on the main beam down in the cabin.

And when Jim Brading asks the Harwich harbourmaster what's happened to the *Goblin*, he's ready to rattle off the details.

My boat. Bermuda cutter. Seven tons, Thames, 4.86 registered. No. 16856.

'Seven tons' as a handy size guide is thus shorthand for her Thames Tonnage

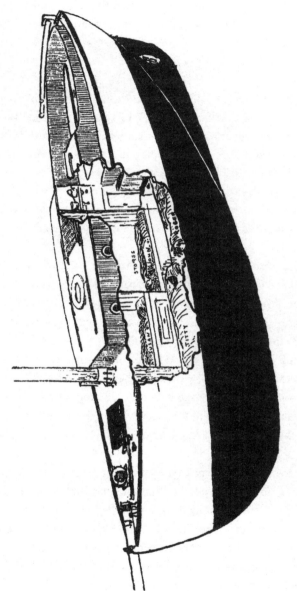

Inside the *Goblin*

which is actually 7.12, arrived at through an arcane formula devised as a way of rating yachts for racing by the Royal Thames Yacht Club in 1855. It uses the following calculation:

$$\frac{(L\text{-}B) \times B \times \frac{1}{2}B}{94}$$

where L = Length (on deck) and B = Beam. These are in Imperial units of course, though a curiosity of the old Certificate of British Registry (the 'Blue Book') is that it records these measurements in feet and tenths of a foot—which makes doing the maths on a calculator a great deal simpler. In *Nancy*'s case the respective dimensions are 28.5ft and 8.1ft. This works out at very nearly 7.12.

Thames tonnage was devised to compensate for excessive overhangs in racing yachts (not a problem with *Nancy*), and to provide a convenient way of rating a boat without having to lift her out of the water. It is derived from Gross Tonnage.

Tonnage, nothing to do with the weight of the ship, is a way of expressing its size through the volume of its supposed cargo capacity. It dates back to the 12th century and Eleanor of Aquitaine, who measured ships by the number of tuns of wine they could carry. 'Gross Tonnage', based on cargo volumes, was introduced by Samuel Plimsoll. In *Nancy*'s case this figure is 6.80 tons—reasonably close to her Thames rating—from which are deducted engine space, 0.44 tons, and 'Chart Space', 1.50 tons, which is carved into a beam towards the aft end of the saloon. The resultant registered tonnage figure of '4.86 registered' was used to determine Light Dues (levied on shipping to pay for lighthouses and buoyage by Trinity House, though not charged on small boats like *Nancy*) and Harbour Dues.

Chart Space is the nominal navigation area, and not the charts themselves which, on *Nancy*, take up no space at all as Ransome, like Jim, kept them under his bunk cushions. It's one of a great many 'allowable deductions' which could be made for non-earning areas of a merchant ship, all of which had to be carved or painted in the relevant part of the vessel. It seems to have become a convenient shorthand when dealing with smaller boats such as *Nancy*, as this entry in Ransome's diary for 4 February 1953, when he was having his second *Lottie Blossom* built at Hillyards, suggests:

Met the Min. Trans. measurer, Mr Chorley, at Littlehampton and was present when he measured the new *Lottie*. I told him we had had no allowances for the first *Lottie*, no galley space, no bosun's stores, etc with the result that her registered tonnage had come out at 5.67, whereas her Thames Tonnage was 5.494. He agreed that this was a bit ridiculous, and in the end, to eliminate unnecessary carving, lumped all allowances together and allowed half the cabin for chart space.

Nancy's Official Number is also carved into her main beam. This is the number issued by the Registrar of British Ships, at her Port of Registry, Littlehampton, and recorded in her Certificate of British Registry (originally a large, cumulatively-inscribed folded document in a hardback linen cover, known as the 'Blue Book', but nowadays a laminated A4 sheet).

Goblin's number is also carved on her main beam, but while her tonnage and *Nancy*'s are identical, their official numbers differ. *Nancy*'s is 162814; *Goblin*'s, as Jim says, is 16856.

Nancy was launched, under the name *Spindrift*, in 1931 by the Littlehampton, Sussex, boatbuilder David Hillyard. She had been commissioned by Seymour Tuely, a retired solicitor from Wimbledon. Her design is described in Hillyard's brochure as a 7-ton auxiliary yacht. Her length on deck is 28ft 6in, plus about 7ft of bowsprit; beam 8ft 2in and draught 4ft 6in. The specification includes pitch pine planking ('carvel laid, in long lengths') copper-fastened on oak timbers, 6in spaced. Oak, 'grown to form' was also used for the stem, sternpost and deadwood, while the keel is listed as elm or oak. Teak was used extensively, for the cabin coamings ('fitted with 6 ports'—two either side and two forward-facing), the cockpit and the deck fittings, rails and covering boards.

Decks were listed as 'Columbian pine, laid in narrow widths, caulked and payed with Marine Glue.' *Nancy*, having been built for exhibition at the Olympia Motor Show, was reputed to have teak decks, but a 1952 survey described them as laid pine. Nowadays the deck is of plywood, finished with non-slip paint, but the original laid planks can clearly be seen in some old photographs, and in some pre-Ransome home-movie footage. The cabin top was, and still is, tongued-and-grooved pine, visible inside, where it is painted white, covered with canvas and non-slip finish outside. Spars were 'pine of good quality, and complete with all

Nancy Blackett ashore, showing her long keel

running and standing gear, as consistent with type'.

The rig offered in the brochure was cutter-style, with a choice of gaff or bermudan mainsail, plus foresail and jib. Roller-reefing is provided for the main, with a crank operated by the famous little brass handle, which John puts in his oilskin pocket as he prepares to go forward and reduce sail; nowadays it lives on a chain beside the mast. For the jib, there's a patented Wykeham Martin self-furling system; no detail is gone into about this in the book, apart from an early mention that 'John had learnt the trick of the rolling jib, and how to make the foot of the staysail fast, and how to clip its hanks onto the forestay.' The staysail, perhaps in the interests of simplicity, gets short shrift during the voyage. It has not been set in the illustration 'All but O.B.' where John, having gone forward to reef, is nearly flung off the foredeck. Nor is it mentioned when John goes to tidy the foredeck in preparation for signalling to the pilot—but it's clearly set in the accompanying illustration.

The engine, which was optional, was the petrol/paraffin Thornycroft 'Handy Billy' DB2. 'Starts first buzz,' Roger tells Daddy. 'At least it did.'

The price, as quoted in Hillyard's brochure for the Olympia Motor Exhibition of 1931, was £535 with engine, £420 without.

David Hillyard, born in 1883, so just a year older than Ransome, had set up his business in around 1906, not long after completing his apprenticeship. By 1931 he had already established a reputation as an innovative builder of wooden boats on mass-production principles, to his own design. This was unusual in the 1920s and 30s, and very different from the usual practice of boatbuilders producing one-offs—either to specifications worked out with the client, or to sets of plans purchased by the client from yacht designers such as T. Harrison Butler, Maurice Griffiths, Laurent Giles and others. The most distinctive Hillyard designs feature a canoe stern, often combined with a centre cockpit, raised to an enclosed wheelhouse in the larger models, but he also produced more conventional boats, like *Nancy*, with transom sterns and aft cockpits, reminiscent of traditional workboats of the era.

He was fussy about the way his boats were built. The element of production-line construction that standard designs permitted enabled costs to be kept down, but he was noted for not skimping on materials: strong oak frames, elm keels, long, thick pitch-pine planks—knot-free below the waterline, as well as a distinctive though unostentatious curve to the sheerline, and a characterisctic gentle camber to the deck and the coachroof.

So it seems improbable that *Nancy*, which displays all these qualities, could be 'only half a Hillyard,' completed on a hull built elsewhere and bought-in. That, however is the persistent rumour attached to her. It comes chiefly from *Nancy*'s second owner, Paget Bowyer, from whom Ransome bought her in 1935.

Ransome was introduced to the boat, then lying in Poole Harbour, and to Bowyer who lived locally, by a Cruising Association acquaintance, William McC. Meek, a naval architect and surveyor of yachts to Lloyd's Register. Meek had previously surveyed the boat (*Spindrift*, as she then was) for Paget Bowyer when he purchased her in 1932. It was he who told Bowyer that her hull, and those of five other boats, had been built by the firm of Shutler's of Poole, and transported by road to Littlehampton.

No reason for such an, on the face of it, unlikely transaction has been uncovered. Was Hillyard overwhelmed with orders and subcontracting work out? Far from it. There was a depression on, and David Hillyard, a principled employer, had been building boats speculatively rather than sack his employees. By 1931 his yard was full of unsold hulls. There is a famous tale of him reluctantly deciding to start dismissals, beginning with the last man taken on. However the man looked so disappointed Hillyard decided to give him a week's reprieve. The following day, a businessman starting a hire fleet in Essex walked into the yard and bought the entire stock.

Was Shutler's in receivership, as has been suggested, with the receiver selling off the hulls? Shutler's did go into receivership at some stage in the '30s, but it's thought towards the end of the decade, not the beginning.

No surviving records at Hillyards support the story, or for that matter contradict it; the firm (which ceased trading in 2009) was notoriously poor at any kind of record-keeping; nor do any members of this close-knit family firm have any recollection of it. But Meek, a respected authority in his day, was firm, and he even gave the names of the resultant boats. In addition to *Nancy* (ex-*Spindrift*) they were: *Fortuna III*, *Magpie*, *Moyune*, *Playmate* and *Riduna II*. These were the names passed on by Paget Bowyer. He added that he had never seen any of them.

Some of these boats are still around—*Fortuna III* and *Moyune* for example—but they shed no light on the mystery.

Nancy's launch date is unrecorded but her Certificate of Registration was issued at Littlehampton on 30 March 1931, under the name of *Spindrift*, and with her owner listed as Seymour Tuely, retired solicitor, of Wimbledon. And it was Tuely's choice of rig, in particular the large bermudan mainsail, that contributes so much to *Nancy*'s distinctive appearance. Initially he combined it with a sloop rig (single foresail, short bowsprit) in contrast to the cutter rig and gaff main which was portrayed in the Hillyard brochure. After one season, he converted her to cutter rig, two foresails, and had a longer bowsprit fitted to accommodate it.

David Hillyard was a firm proponent of gaff rig, then virtually the norm except among racing yachts. However, he was also a businessman, and as his brochure shows, was prepared—with reluctance—to offer the option of bermudan for customers who wanted it.

Tuely's son-in-law Norman Morley, de facto co-owner of *Spindrift*, wrote:

> Dave had grave objections to this, on the grounds that the slides always jammed in the track causing endless trouble. However, as we were determined, he suggested the cross-trees be set as high as possible, mast hoops up to that height and the upper part of the sail hanked to a wire jackstay, running from top to bottom of the mast, inside the mast hoops and set up bar taught with a rigging screw. This method was adopted and I would mention in passing that however taut the jackstay, the head invariably sagged away from the mast.

Although *Nancy*'s next owner, Paget Bowyer, switched to a mast track, Ransome reverted to hoops and jackstay—as climbed by John in *We Didn't Meant to Go to Sea*, 'hoop by hoop as if he were climbing a ladder', and depicted in the illustration 'On the Cross-trees'. This is the system *Nancy* now has, except that the jackstay is tensioned by the halyard that hauls it through the mast-head and down.

Tuely and Morley were also responsible for the compass porthole which Susan decided was in need of polishing. They found the idea in a book by yachting writer Francis B. Cooke, who suggests that it enables the compass to be kept inside out of the weather where its candle light is less likely to blow out.

Tuely and Morley kept *Spindrift* for only a couple of seasons, selling her back to Hillyards in December 1932. They resold her quite quickly, in February 1933, to the young Paget Bowyer, a 'student of engineering' according to the Blue Book, who changed her name to *Electron*—he wanted something modern and, as he told me towards the end of his life, 'They were the days of splitting the atom.'

'A horrible name,' according to Ransome, who does not even deign to record it in an unpublished section of his autobiography.

Ransome also described her as 'little-used', a phrase picked up by Hugh Brogan in his biography, and to which Bowyer took strong exception—Brogan now thinks the phrase may have originated with the broker. Bowyer kept her in Poole Harbour, at Rum Row, and sailed her every year to Falmouth, as well as more locally at weekends. Soon after buying her, he sailed her into Yarmouth, IoW, in a strong squall, and broke her bowsprit on the stern of Lord Melchett's boat. 'I left next day for Lymington and got Berthon to make a new one, but 9ft instead of 6ft.' The mast track came in 1935 when he had a suit of white sails made.

Ransome, whose address was still Low Ludderburn, Windermere, when the sale was recorded (and whose profession is given as 'Author'), travelled down to Poole on Sunday 8 September 1935, with Meek, who appears to have been acting both as his adviser and Bowyer's agent. He saw the boat and promptly bought her, after an unsuccessful attempt at haggling, for the asking price £525. The money came from the sale of Low Ludderburn.

Following his wild but inspiring delivery trip from Poole, Ransome made something of a ceremony of his arrival. 'I had set my heart on coming into Harwich in daylight for the first time,' so he extended the journey to the Sunk lightship, and hung about for a while.

At dawn, we let draw and for the first time I enjoyed, as I always do enjoy it, the entry into Harwich harbour and the sail up the river to Pin Mill. Through the trees to starboard as we sailed, I could see the roof of the house that was to be ours, and presently we picked up a mooring off Pin Mill and went ashore to the Butt and Oyster and to see Mr King in whose charge I had arranged to leave the boat. Mr King flattered me very much by saying that he had made sure we should not have left Poole, and would be waiting there for rather better weather. As he says, 'You couldn't have chosen worse.' It has been very uncomfortable but at least it has shown me that Meek had found me a wonderful little boat.

Ransome lived aboard *Nancy* on her new mooring at Pin Mill while Broke Farm (their new home at Levington, across the river) was being sorted out. Then, after a few short, local sails, *Nancy* was laid up, in a mud-berth, for the winter. Ransome had her gear brought round to Broke Farm and 'had a happy time in the attic scraping and varnishing blocks, painting lanterns, greasing wire rigging, making up halyards and getting through all those other small jobs that make the care of a boat so satisfying an occupation.' Sometimes he would go and sit aboard *Nancy*, and light her stove to dry her out, or sail his dinghy *Coch-y-bonddhu* which he'd had sent down from Windermere. Indeed he could combine the two occupations—sailing *Cocky* the mile-and-a-half upriver from Levington to Pin Mill was a more attractive option than the twelve-mile road trip via Ipswich (no Orwell Bridge in those days).

'Pin Mill is the best anchorage on the whole of the East Coast,' he wrote, 'and when spring came there were always the little ships of our friends coming in for a day or two before going on elsewhere. With a spy glass from my window I could often recognise a boat coming in, and be expecting the telephone when on reaching Pin Mill somebody got ashore.'

They included the Young family, the Wandsworth brewers, 'a young and happy crew' up from Maldon 'in a Blackwater smack, flying the skull and crossbones and firing off guns by way of a salute.' There were the 'redoubtable' Miss Wiles of *Cocquette* (and later *Keryl*) who won cups for cruising; the Taylors (he had invented the CQR anchor, for which Ransome was immensely grateful—its lightness in effect allowed him to sail *Nancy* where a conventional fisherman's would have been too much); Bos'sun Walker of *Deerfoot*, Herbert Hanson of the Cruising Association, the Busk family, who were to appear in Secret Water—and P. G. Rouse 'whom I had last met when we were boys at Rugby', and who became a regular crew for *Nancy*.

There were also plenty of 'web-footed children' around. Taqui Altounyan, then aged 18, was at school not far away. The eldest daughter of his friends Ernest and Dora, she was one of the four for whom *Swallows and Amazons* was written,

Arthur Ransome, and cat, at the gate of Broke Farm, Levington

and indeed on whom the Swallows were based (more or less—the others were indeed Susan, Titty and Roger and while literary convention demanded the eldest be a boy, John, much of Taqui's personality resurfaced in Nancy Blackett). Ransome wrote to her in October 1935: 'I very much want you to see her [*Nancy*] before we put her to bed. I have been hard at work in her all day, finishing off the dreadful bad splices left by previous owners. She is beautifully dry, but the Turkey carpet is all over fluff from bad rope ends. You'd better come along and do some brushing.' (The same Turkey carpet, incidentally, turned up on my doorstep, sixty-odd years later).

Then there were Josephine and George Russell. They had just moved into Broke Hall, to which Ransome's home had been the home farm, when they met him on the shore of Levington Creek one afternoon, pulling up his dinghy. They lent a hand, chatted a while and, as they parted, he said, 'By the way, my name's Ransome.' 'Could it be...?' wondered Josephine, a fan of the books. Somewhat to her surprise, and even more to her brother's, who had dismissed the idea, it was. A firm friendship sprang up and they quickly graduated to regular crew. ('George & Jos. V. good as crew, but must learn to make ropes fast after hauling in,' Ransome noted in his log, 24 April 1937, after taking them for a sail and making them late for the circus). George was a serious boy, near-sighted and bespectacled, rather like Dick Callum (and Ransome himself, as a boy); Josephine was lively and enthusiastic, and she is credited with taking a good many of the surviving photographs of that era. George was killed in the Second World War; Josephine, still with us when we bought *Nancy*, was a vigorous old lady, enthusiastic and supportive, and deservedly until her death in 2008 a vice-president of the Nancy Blackett Trust.

And there were the Pin Mill residents, the Kings of course, the boatbuilding dynasty whose firm is still there today; Miss Powell, who kept Alma Cottage as a guest house—and had to learn to make pea soup and omelettes after Ransome ascribed them to her in *We Didn't Mean to Go to Sea*, and her brother John Powell, 'practical sail maker and ship chandler' whose loft was the little shop at the Butt and Oyster end of Alma Terrace.

For Ransome, Pin Mill, at the bottom of its 'deep green lane that ended in the river itself... this happy place where almost everybody wore sea-boots and land, in comparison with water, seemed hardly to matter at all,' was the perfect spot to rediscover his joy of sailing—and for the start of an adventure. How could he not put it into a book?

CHAPTER THREE

Sailing and Writing

૭ᵔ

Ransome mostly went for short, local sails in *Nancy*, frequently to the Walton Backwaters, just down the coast from Pin Mill, where he might stop over-night. He would take *Cocky* with him on these trips, and slip away for a sail in her when he should have been working aboard *Nancy*. He relished getting to know both the boat and the area—his exuberance is captured in a letter to his mother in August 1936:

> ...we had the best run I've had since coming home to Riga in the gale back in 1922. With the storm sails she was quite happy, and fairly flew, big waves picking her up and she riding the top of them in a flurry of white foam until they passed her and she slipped down to be picked up by the next. It really was gorgeous. We did not see any other yachts on the whole passage, just one steamship and two barges, which looked very fine indeed. The three of us, the two big Thames barges and my little *Nancy*, all came storming round the Naze together.

He did however make one major voyage in each of the three years he owned *Nancy*. In 1936, it was to Flushing, in order to research the *Goblin*'s trip in *We Didn't Mean to Go to Sea*. He set off on 1 June with, for crew, an oddly timid young man called Herbert-Smith who clearly hadn't grasped the purpose of the trip. As Ransome's log puts it:

> Started from Shotley under power 12.30. Bar 29.8 steady. Wind variable. Headed us getting out. Beating against it Felixstowe to Landguard. Stopped engine. Comfortable under full main & jib. Mate urging Brightlingsea!!!!! & jetissoning plan of going to Holland.

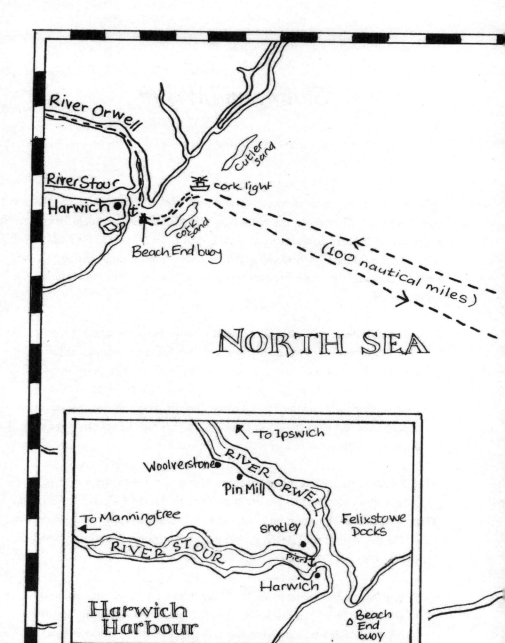

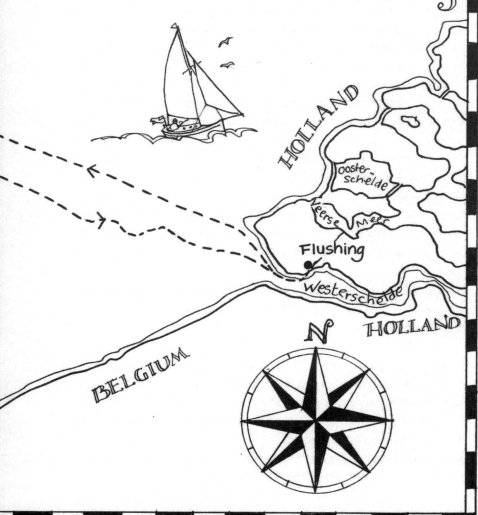

Voyage of
Nancy Blackett/Goblin
Harwich - Flushing

HOLLAND

Ooster-schelde

Veerse Meer

Flushing

Westerschelde

HOLLAND

BELGIUM

N

Later when they passed the Galloper lightship, with a forecast of light westerlies,

> Mate then said 'If she was mine I'd put about now. We ought to be making for the
> coast Yarmouth or Lowestoft way.'

Ransome appears to have helmed for the vast majority of the twenty-five-hour, ninety-three-mile passage, rather as John does in the *Goblin*. They made Flushing lock at 1.30 the following afternoon, and moored up 'to post on port hand in the canal. V. comfortable berth barring small boys who in the end behaved all right.'

The following day they motored up the canal to Middelburg and Veere, where the mate (for all his shortcomings) 'gallantly bought a tile for *Nancy*', and back again, tying up a little above their previous berth. Ransome didn't bother to take a pilot coming into Flushing, but he soon met one, whose boat, Pilot Vessel No 7, was moored up close to *Nancy*. This was E. de Smit (apprentice), who became a good friend ('Coffee with Pilot de Smit and his wife in their v. clean and jolly little kitchen. Rowed off in dinghy & photographed his pilot steamer, No7.')

Ransome was held back by the weather, and eventually paid off his use-less crewman, who had been caught out lying to the Pilot about his experience. De Smit then introduced him to a capable young Dutchman, Goer, who would ship for the passage home for £1 a day and his return fare.

> We had supper together & he seemed very pleasant, but inclined to imagine he was
> wanted to 'take' us across. I explained that I wanted to 'take' myself. He was all
> right on that point.

They left on 9 June, clearing the lock at 5pm and coming back via Zeebrugge and Ostend, rather than the *Goblin*'s straight reverse-bearing, with the option of making for Dover if the wind continued in the north-west. Soon after passing the Ruytingen light vessel, the wind 'did as asked and went SW. We delightedly gave up Dover, and laid a course for the Sunk.'

Soon after dawn on 12 June, the Cork light vessel showed up 'like a ghost' in the mist. 'Then,' records Ransome, 'we saw a lovelier ghost, the four-masted barque *Pommern* being towed out.' The sighting is replicated in the illustration

Ransome and *Nancy* at Waldringfield, on the Deben

'Meeting the sailing ship' in *We Didn't Mean to Go to Sea*, where it becomes a sort of symbolic blessing on the *Goblin*'s voyage.

The following year, 1937, Ransome invited Philip (P. G.) Rouse to accompany him on a week-long voyage. Rouse and Ransome had been contemporaries at Rugby school. They hadn't met again for forty years, but the previous year Rouse, by then a naval architect, had sailed his small gaffer *Mermaid* into the Orwell and brought up close to *Nancy*, with Ransome aboard. Their friendship was quickly rekindled, and Rouse—'by long chalks the pleasantest companion and the best crew *Nancy* has had'—frequently sailed with Ransome. On this occasion, Rouse having arranged a week's leave from work, Ransome decided to let the wind determine the destination. 'I had told him that if the wind on the Saturday was westerly, we should go to Holland; if easterly, we should go down Channel.'

They left Pin Mill on the Friday night, 14 May, and anchored off Felixstowe. In the morning, the wind was hard north-east, and a friend on a neighbouring boat reported a bad forecast. 'We decided at least to go out and let *Nancy* see how she liked it. We left Harwich harbour and she liked it very well.' They reached Portsmouth late on the Monday and anchored under Portchester Castle, where Ransome had visited his friend Herbert Hanson, on Hanson's *Ianthe*, the previous October ('a real fairy story castle'). Their main concern while there was to track down some instructions for a new pressure-cooker, and some meat to cook in it. Then the wind swung round to the west, and on Thursday they set off for home, arriving back at Pin Mill on the Saturday, 'in time for the tail-end of a sausage and shanty party at the Butt and Oyster.'

Ransome wrote up this 'extraordinarily pleasant and lucky little cruise' for the *Bulletin* of the Cruising Association, of which he had been a member since his *Racundra* days, when he was Honorary Port Officer at Reval; later he was to help keep the association going through World War II. The article, *Saturday to Saturday*, is reproduced here as Interlude 1.

The voyage reconfirmed his already high opinion of his boat. '*Nancy* is a good little boat, considering that she was built as a cruiser not a racer and is so comfortable that a man can spend months on end in her.'

The 1938 trip was more modest. With Rouse again, he took *Nancy* down to Burnham and Brightlingsea, and up to Orford and Lowestoft.

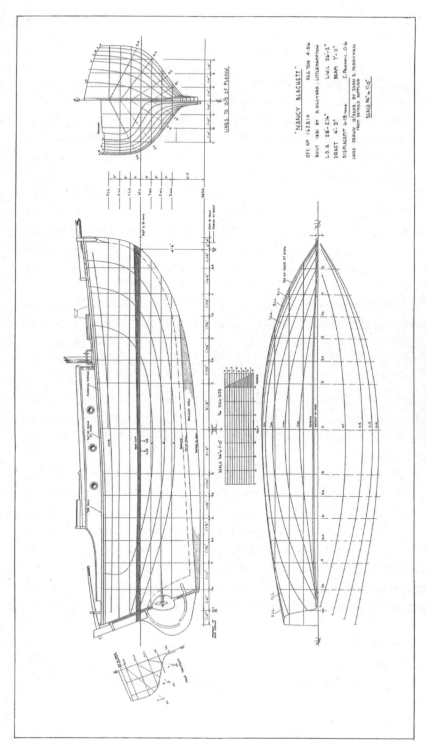

Lines of *Nancy Blackett*, drawn by John Perryman

Between these trips, apart from the occasional *Cocky* truancy in the Backwaters, Ransome was working hard on *We Didn't Mean to Go to Sea*, and on other literary tasks. Although the idea for the book came to him in January 1936, and he made a synopsis, he was still working on the illustrations for *Swallows and Amazons* and *Swallowdale*, to replace those by Clifford Webb, and gearing himself up to start revising the draft of *Pigeon Post*. In the end, according to the unpublished part of his autobiography, he 'rewrote it entirely, finishing on the last day of July.' He left the manuscript for Evgenia to read and, with Rouse, sailed off in *Nancy* for a long weekend. Getting back to Pin Mill, 'I went ashore and telephoned nervously to hear the verdict of the Critic on the hearth. 'Not much worse than the worst of the others.' This was much better than I had expected and we celebrated in hot rum.'

After that there were the pictures and a final revision. 'Final proofs went to the printers in October, and I began at once on *We Didn't Mean to Go to Sea*.' Writing the book took up 'much of 1937... either in *Nancy* or at Broke Farm'.

In June of that year, Evgenia came for one of her rare sails. 'Object was for Genia to see how she could manage with the anchor,' records Ransome's log. In this respect it was a bit of a failure. 'Genia went to sleep in the cabin. Walton buoy 12.15. Genia heard the splash as the anchor went o.b. and thought it was me, but did not come up to look, and was much surprised when I came to tell her we were already anchored.'

A couple of days later the first draft of *We Didn't Mean to Go to Sea* was finished, and Evgenia was left to read it while Ransome took himself off in *Nancy*. 'June 15. Single-handed while Genia reading my damned book.' The sail was problematic: 'Violent northerly wind at Pin Mill and I rather did myself in pulling off against it in heavy shore boat of Burrough's. Had to stop half way as making no progress. Hung on to anchored boat for a few minutes.' Despite harsh weather—and presumably only because he wanted to keep clear of Genia while she was reading the manuscript—he made it to Brightlingsea and, two days later, back.

Picked up my mooring at Pin Mill at 4.30 too dead beat to stow. Had some tinned herrings and fell asleep. Waked up later on, stowed sails, washed deck, and so home to hear the sad news that my book had a good skeleton but was dead, flat, nowhere amusing, no dialogue, no characters, and not interesting. I asked were there any good spots and was told No. But next day she had remembered two paragraphs that were fit to pass.

Fortunately, Molly Hamilton, an old friend and a more constructive critic, visited and read the draft, making helpful suggestions, such as enlarging Titty's role (always a good idea, but probably something of a challenge at the time). It was she who suggested deferring the explanation of Jim's absence until towards the end.

Ransome worked away on revising the book, although in July he suffered violent duodenal trouble while sailing. Eventually Evgenia's approval was sufficient and *We Didn't Mean to Go to Sea* went to the printers on 15 September 1937, in time for publication in November of the same year. In October the Ransomes took themselves off to the Broads and a hired motor cruiser, to use as a 'moveable houseboat' and do some fishing, but the holiday was interrupted by the eruption of an umbilical hernia, which required operation. Ransome was worried it might mean he could not sail again, but was reassured that he would be 'not merely as good as new, but better'.

This was just as well, because they had just decided to build a boat for themselves, 'one in which G, best of sea-cooks, should have the galley she deserved'. This was *Selina King*, built by King's, the Pin Mill boatbuilders, and launched in September 1938.

Nancy Blackett was sold on 7 December—though the *Goblin* was to sail on a little longer.

CHAPTER FOUR

A Serious Kind of Joy

❧

If Ransome really didn't know where his next book was coming from after *Pigeon Post*, as seems to be the case, then the idea supplied by Nancy Blackett and, perhaps subconsciously, by the dramatic delivery voyage that had made him feel so 'young and inexperienced' was an absolute corker. Not only did it provide a thrilling adventure narrative, it also achieved a hitherto-untapped level of emotional intensity that added a new dimension and dynamic to the whole series.

We Didn't Mean to Go to Sea, unlike the other books in the series, is rich in symbolism. At the same time, and again unlike the preceding books, it is totally bereft of anything resembling game-playing or fantasy. The reason for that is obvious enough: this is the real thing. No longer are the Swallows (shouldn't they be called the Goblins now?) pootling about in a dinghy on an inland lake, inventing fantasy wars and expeditions. They are at sea, in a deficiently-equipped yacht, coping with all that the weather can throw at them, not to mention other vessels, the uncertainties of venturing into foreign territory and above all their own fears and inexperience.

Peter Hunt, professor of children's literature, in his book *Approaching Arthur Ransome*, points out that 'as in a fairy tale' the children receive various specific gifts. These take the form of advice, warnings and training, imparted by Jim Brading as the *Goblin* sails down the River Orwell.

''Better learn the ropes,' Jim had said', and he teaches the Walker children—and John in particular—how to hoist the mainsail, and reef it with the little brass handle, the trick of the rolling jib, and how to set the staysail. He gives John, and then Susan, the helm, and explains about buoyage and sound signals, from both ships and buoys. He warns them, very emphatically, about the risks of going aground—'easily lose the boat'—and of longshore sharks claiming it for salvage. He demonstrates how the torch can be shone through a red Woolworth's plate (just as Ransome himself had done, in his maiden voyage aboard *Nancy*)—'Good as a port light'. He shows where the charts live, under the port bunk. At John's request he uses one of them to point out the shoals off Harwich, and repeats his mantra: 'Only one motto for the *Goblin*. When in doubt keep clear of shoals… get out to sea and stay there.'

Ransome takes the opportunity to drop a couple of hints as to what's to come. 'John listened, telling himself that he too would have that motto, when at last he should have a ship of his own.' Then, when they go ashore to get water and phone Mother at the pub in Shotley, 'They had come only a few miles from Pin Mill, but it felt like landing in a different country.' And once more, at bedtime: 'For a few minutes John stood in the cockpit alone. Almost the *Goblin* might have been his own ship…' Little does he realise that within 24 hours she will in effect be exactly that.

What Hunt doesn't mention is that while he is loading his protagonists with useful skills, Ransome is also quietly depriving them of some of the essentials of being at sea—and has been doing so from the very beginning of the book. The red and green navigation lights ran out of oil on Jim's passage from Dover. It's the engine's running out of petrol that deprives them of both that assistance and their skipper. Then John loses one anchor and fails to get the other one down before they have drifted irretrievably out of the harbour.

Now they, and John in particular, have to put into use all the sailing skills they've acquired, not only over the last day or so, but over the years.

In short, it's a coming-of-age novel, and a remarkably deft and satisfying one. The Beach End buoy is not simply marking the division between the river and the open sea; it signifies the end of childhood and the beginning of growing up. In passing it, they have—whether they meant to or not—passed out of the sheltered realm of parental care and into the wide world where they must fend for themselves.

Ransome piles detail on detail. Tides. Charts. Rigging. Every item becomes an urgent problem, part of the puzzle they must unlock or unravel to keep sailing safely.

Much is made of the promise to Mother, and—particularly by Susan—of the awful fact of their having broken it. But in truth, it has been broken for them, and all they can do is cope with the consequences. John instinctively recognises this the moment he decides he must get some sail on her. 'It's the only thing to do. We're helpless, drifting like this.' Susan, who has always been the mother-figure in the camps and the adventures, clings on to the idea of repairing the promise as their primary objective. 'If you're sure land's over there, why not go straight for it and get ashore somehow or other?' With those last few words, we know already she's—literally—out of her depth.

> 'We can't,' said John. 'We'd only wreck the *Goblin*...'
>
> 'I believe we ought,' said Susan.
>
> 'We can't,' said John, almost angrily. 'Go and look at that chart. We might easily hit rocks ever so far out from the shore, and in the fog we wouldn't know which way to swim.'
>
> 'Mother'd be wanting us to try...'
>
> 'I don't believe she would... And Daddy wouldn't anyway. Look here, Susan. So long as the *Goblin*'s all right, we're all right.'

This short but crucial episode contains the kernel of the forthcoming experience—a journey into new waters both actual and emotional. Ransome hasn't hitherto really done emotion in his children's books. It's often there, under the surface, but apart from Nancy's explosions of anger—frequently at her long-suffering uncle, or inanimate objects such as the 'beastly Arctic'—it's conveyed obliquely and delicately. John's buttoned-up response after his encounter with the 'houseboat man' in *Swallows and Amazons*. The Swallows' coolness towards the D's when they suspect them of wrecking the Arctic expedition in *Winter Holiday*. Titty's inner wrestlings over her dowsing abilities in *Pigeon Post*.

But here we have John, under pressure, almost losing his temper, and Susan totally losing her capable, managing 'Susanish' demeanour. In the event, John, buoyed by the conviction that he's doing the right thing, remains calm and in control. For him, the right course of action is confirmed by the chart, which shows 'what looked like a broad, clear road leading out to deep water between the threatening shoals.'

It's Susan, still clinging to the past, and the promise to Mother, worrying about the effect the disappearance of the *Goblin* might even then be having on Jim and on Mother, and unable to reconcile it with what John knows is the only thing they can do, who goes to pieces. Her hopelessly conflicted emotional state is underlined by her seasickness and, when John eventually agrees to turn the *Goblin* round and try for home, is externalised into the gale that, now they are facing into it, flings her against the cockpit as the *Goblin* dives into breaking seas, with water sluicing across her decks as John struggles to regain control.

> John, white-faced and desperate but still thinking how they were to get back, tried to see the swinging compass, to ease the mainsheet, and to steer against a force that was too much for him.
>
> 'Stop it, John! Stop it!'
>
> 'I can't…. I can't…. Ough!…. Oughgulloch…. Ough… Oh!…. Oh…!'
>
> And Susan, shaken almost to pieces with this new violent motion of the battling ship, lay half across the cockpit, with her head across the coaming and was sick. A wave broke across the cabin roof and a lump of green water hit her on the side of the head.

Rarely if ever does Ransome inflict such punishment on one of his characters (the seasick groans and gulps, incidentally, are vividly rendered in the audiobook version by Gabriel Woolf). It reinforces the very real peril that they now find themselves in. And the cure for seasickness, when it comes, is almost worse than the malady itself. John, who has left Susan at the helm and gone forward to reef the mainsail, slips on the deck and almost goes overboard. Susan lets out a shriek of terror… but it's alright. John recovers himself ('Susan never knew the effort it cost him to stand up once more, just for a moment, so as not to feel himself beaten.') and makes his way back to the cockpit, full of reassurance.

> 'Nothing happened,' said John. 'I slipped. The lifeline worked beautifully. I'd have been all right even if I had gone overboard.' With hands that shook a little in spite of nothing having happened, he untied the rope he had knotted round his middle, coiled it carefully and put it away in the rope locker.
>
> Titty, climbing out, looked from John to Susan and from Susan to John. She

All but O. B.

was just going to ask a question, but did not ask it. She felt that the ship was suddenly full of happiness. John was grinning to himself. Susan was smiling through
tears that did not seem to matter.

In a very original and perceptive examination of *We Didn't Mean to Go to Sea*
which David Chan, a New Zealand Ransome fan sent me (a version was later
published in the Arthur Ransome Society's journal *Mixed Moss*), he suggests that
in addition to their status as individual characters, Susan and John represent two
parts of a single character struggling to resolve the dilemma which their situation presents them with. His thesis delves into psychology and mythology—both
areas that may be unfamiliar territory for some readers of the books, though not
entirely alien from the world of folk tales.

This 'single personality' might equally be regarded as a single problem which
is the central dilemma in any rite-of-passage/coming-of-age situation: to go forward (into the unknown) or to go back (to parental protection and the comfortable certainties of childhood). All Ransome is doing, it might be argued, is re-
cruiting two of his characters to carry the two sides of the argument. This would
perhaps not entirely satisfy Chan: he goes on to posit the idea that the modern
male psyche has become 'disjointed', emphasising *logos*, the thinking and reasoning side, at the expense of *eros* the feeling, imaginative, unconscious, feminine
side. As he writes, 'Men typically cannot bear to face the ambiguity and uncertainty of emotions and rush into 'clarity' by the imposition of reason and logic.'

John brings to the situation the male thinking and reasoning exemplified
by his male role models. 'What was the right thing to do? What would Jim do?
What would Jim think he ought to do?' he asks himself (a fascinating triple
question, each testing in a slightly different way the same answer). And when
Susan suggests 'Mother'd be wanting us to try' (to turn back), he replies 'I don't
believe she would... And Daddy wouldn't, anyway.' It's noteworthy that in addition to invoking Daddy, as the clincher to the argument, John also ascribes to
Mother the same view. Whether he's right or not is an interesting question. As
a grown-up with a reasonable amount of relevant experience she probably would
have supported Daddy's, and John's, view, but as the later chapter 'At Pin Mill'
shows she would not have done so without the anxiety that Susan is sharing.

Chan makes the point that in agreeing to turn back, 'John is facing completely his internal [feminine] emotional state. He does not merely ignore what Susan wants and insist that the rational, detached, masculine way (ie to sail on in the same direction) is the only way.' One consequence of this is that as a result of the experience, it is Susan who agrees that they must carry on, and, despite a little wobble when they see the steamer, throws herself fully into the enterprise.

As Chan puts it, 'the book has several layers of meaning, some of which are more apparent than others'. Some readers, indeed, may dismiss some of the more advanced aspects of his argument altogether (I'm not entirely convinced by all of them myself). But the fact that the book is capable of being mined for these concepts, and of being subjected to this degree of analysis, is, I think, a testament to the power of its themes and its treatment. The pattern of the story, with its preparation, its conflicts, both with the sea and among the crew, its crisis and the aftermath of these as the quest is completed, is in fact pure folk tale, the traditional vehicle for conveying all manner of psychological conflicts and challenges.

That was an area Ransome knew something about—he went to Russia initially to study them, and produced *Old Peter's Russian Tales*—and valued highly, though this seems to be the only solid example of its influence within the *S&A* series. (There are glimpses elsewhere of course—*Peter Duck* is a sort of deconstructed quest—and in Ransome's autobiography the account of his crossing no-man's land with his typewriter and his pipe, his rescue of Evgenia and the various chances, ruses and gifts that facilitate their escape, is given a very folk-tale flavour.)

Here, in *We Didn't Mean to Go to Sea*, the arrival on the scene of Daddy, chiefly to legitimise the quest, has a particularly strong folk element. A lot of readers find his turning up in the way that it is described a weak point in the narrative, and Ransome's deliberate cutting between scenes, in a very filmic way, to introduce uncertainty—has the boat sailed when the figure of Daddy is espied still dodging between passengers on the lower deck? —tends, paradoxically, to underline the improbability. But it's Ransome's skill to make the improbable seem inevitable, and that is what he does here.

For Chan, 'it is the connection between John and his father that is the epiphanous moment of the book, the emotional climax that gives meaning to the journey through the storm.'

Brogan too, in the *Life*, leaps to the conclusion that this is the climax of the book: 'As his letter announcing its conception makes plain, the climax of the turbulent voyage was from the first to be the meeting with the children's father.'

Actually, the letter—to Wren Howard, his editor at Jonathan Cape—isn't all that plain. It speaks of 'a first-class climax inevitable and handed out on a plate', but doesn't describe it any further. It's perhaps reasonable to conclude that this was what Ransome had in mind, and Brogan also links it to the relationship between Ransome and his father Cyril. 'In *We Didn't Mean to Go to Sea* he at last confronted the ghost of Cyril Ransome.'

Cyril, who died when Arthur was 13—not far short of the age of John in the book—had always been an emotionally distant father to whom young Arthur felt he was a constant disappointment. Brogan concludes: 'His daydream of at last earning and winning the approval that had been so rigidly withheld had at length given him the theme for a book of which Conrad would have been proud.'

This may well be true: the circumstantial inevitability of their crossing Commander Walker's path has been carefully built up and is a necessary element of the narrative. Although it has to be said that Daddy is no Cyril Ransome: geographically distant a lot of the time, yes, but emotionally warm, cheerful and encouraging. The meeting is certainly a climactic moment in the second half of the book.

> 'A lot of things were lucky,' said Daddy, and suddenly, while they were walking along, brought his hand down on John's shoulder and gave it a bit of a squeeze. 'You'll be a seaman yet, my son.' And John, for one dreadful moment, felt that something was going wrong with his eyes. A sort of wetness, and hotness... Partly salt... Pleased though he was, he found himself biting his lower lip pretty hard, and looking the other way.

This, together with Daddy's frequent habit of addressing John as 'Skipper', is certainly a measure of parental approval that Ransome may have been subconsciously seeking for his younger self. But is it *the* climax? Ransome may have intended it as such in the planning of the book, plotted it as a waymark to be navigated towards, and made the most of the scene's emotional impact when he got to it. But things change in the writing and by the time he came to write the *Goblin*'s night passage across the North Sea, the event itself, and its significance had quite overtaken the need for its approval by any adult.

The most significant relationship in the book for John is not with his father, nor even with his sister, important though the resolution of their conflict is. It is with his ship, as he realises early on in the voyage. 'So long as the *Goblin*'s all right, we're all right.' And it is when he loses faith in his own seamanship, and accedes to Susan's desire to turn the *Goblin* round, that things immediately go wrong. It's significant that, once the incident is over, and the *Goblin* is back on her course, the book found floating in the water in the cabin should be the now-becoming-outgrown *Knight on Sailing*.

From then on, John's confidence in his own judgment grows. He manages to reef without mishap (just), and avoids being run down by the steamer. It is a nice touch to interject the flashback to Mother and Bridget at Pin Mill just at this point. We see Mother first anxious, then reassured. She is totally mistaken in the belief from which she derives that comfort, but we know that she is right.

And it is in the very next chapter that the true climax of the book is sealed and celebrated. The rest of the crew is asleep, John is back at the tiller:

> He took another look at the compass card under that dim yellow glow, wedged himself against the cockpit coaming with a foot against the opposite seat, looked up at the part of the sky that was full of stars, and a little ashamedly admitted to himself that he was happy.

Ransome's old friend John Masefield could hardly put it more poetically, or more economically. The technical check, the fitting of body to boat, the sense of one's place in the universe, and the slightly-tempered sense of relief and satisfaction. For John knows

> He had done his very best. And anyhow, here, at night, far out in the North Sea, what could he do other than what he was doing? If anybody could have seen his face in the faint glimmer from the compass window, he would have seen that there was a grin on it. For John was alone in the dark with his ship.

The Beach End Buoy

And it is this, the bonding between the sailor and his ship, that is the crux of the novel. For John, it is the coming-of-age, the rite of passage, the transition from boyhood to manhood. And it is a bond that transcends any unfinished business between the schoolboy Arthur and his cold father, or indeed between John and his own father. Later on, Daddy might tell him that he will, some time in the future, be a seaman. Right now, John knows he is a seaman and takes a moment to relish it.

> He for that night was the Master of the *Goblin*, and even the lurches of the cockpit beneath him as the *Goblin* rushed through the dark filled him with a serious kind of joy. He and the *Goblin* together. On and on. On and on. Years and years hence, when he was grown up, he would have a ship of his own and sail her out into wider seas than this. But he would always and always remember the night when for the first time ship and crew were in his charge and his alone.
>
> So… and back… So… and back… Lean and sway with this triumphant motion. Good little ship. Good little ship. He put a hand over the edge of the coaming and patted the damp deck in the darkness.

The significance of John's achievement, and the source of that 'serious kind of joy', was summed up by Ransome many years later, when he was writing a foreword to R. T. McMullen's *Down Channel* for the *Mariners Library*. McMullen, the original source of Jim's advice to 'Get out to sea and stay there', was a favourite writer, whom Ransome described thus:

> In his writings, for the first time, yachting ceased to be a sort of social ceremony dependent largely on the presence of spectators, but an affair between man and nature, a series of trials in which the prize to be attained is that a man shall stand well with himself. No winning guns or spectators' smiles matter in the least. In these contests a man is his own judge and, in secret, at least, a strict one.

John's maturity had advanced to the stage that not only had he done the right thing, but he could recognise, and acknowledge to himself, that this was so, and Ransome rightly celebrates this, with that pat of the 'good little ship's' damp deck in the darkness.

CHAPTER FIVE

A Postcard from Arthur Ransome: 'Eight are about enough'

એ

One of the very good reasons for preserving and displaying any kind of anti-quarian artefact is that simply by being there it can generate new knowledge and understanding about its subject—by unlocking memories or attracting other items out of 'retirement'. So it has been with *Nancy Blackett*. In November 2004, the Trust received a gift which cast a whole new light on Ransome's intentions for the *Swallows and Amazons* series, and suggested that it might well have ended up at only two-thirds of its actual length.

From time to time, people make us donations of books, by Arthur Ransome and others, often quite valuable ones, which we auction to raise funds. It's unusu-al though to get a near-complete *S&A* set including a number of first editions, but this is what we were given by a lady in Edinburgh who had collected them when she was a girl, buying, or being given, many of the titles as they came out. The most significant item, though, was pasted inside *Secret Water*, one of the first edi-tions. It was a card from Arthur Ransome, evidently written in response to a fan letter from the young owner. Ransome had a supply of these cards printed, with a generous border featuring some of his drawings, and leaving a smallish blank area in the centre which it would not be too taxing for him to fill with an individual reply to letters from young admirers.

This one, dated 6 February 1940, just four months after the book's publica-tion, reads: 'Thank you for your nice letter. I am glad you like the books. I'll have to see what can be done about another, though it seems to me that eight are about enough. Best wishes for fair winds, Arthur Ransome'.

Whether Ransome ever seriously intended to stop with *Secret Water*, we may never know. He often felt—particularly just after publication—that his latest book was his last and he couldn't do it again, or he may simply have been teasing. But it makes an intriguing subject for speculation. There is a certain shape to the series of twelve books, with the two Broads books; the two fantasies, *Peter Duck* and *Missee Lee*; plus *The Picts and the Martyrs*, which by including the Blacketts and the Callums but not the Swallows in a way balances the Swallows-only *We Didn't Mean to Go to Sea*, and then, in *Great Northern*, everybody together in a grand—and, I've always thought, well-managed—finale.

If Ransome had indeed decided to stop at eight, the shape of the series would have been very different, and so would its emphasis, but it would, I feel, have been no less satisfying, and arguably more so. If we think about just the first eight books, and try to ignore the subsequent four, it's easy to see in them a developmental arc which is all about the Swallows. It begins with them getting permission from Daddy to go sailing in a dinghy on a lake, in what becomes for them a voyage of exploration to an unknown island. It ends (or almost ends) with them sailing a real ship across a real ocean, to a truly unknown land. They are sailing at night, and without permission, though none of this is their fault, and—in contrast to the night-sailing escapade in *Swallows and Amazons*—they are not the least dufferish. Indeed, the voyage ends with the appearance of Daddy, who bestows his approval.

That, of course, is all in *We Didn't Mean to Go to Sea*, which is the seventh book of the eight. So what exactly is *Secret Water* for, and how does it fit in to this supposed pattern? Well, one of the things many Ransome readers remark on in his books are his 'lulls'—periods where nothing much seems to be happening, but which serve to deepen the reader's involvement with the characters and their situation, and give space for reflection on what has happened previously. *Secret Water*, in which the *Goblin* makes a brief reappearance, at the beginning and again at the end, can be regarded as a mega-lull, a reflective coda to the high drama of *We Didn't Mean to Go to Sea*. But there is much more going on under the surface. Compare the plot for a moment with *Swallows and Amazons*. Once again the Walker children are being given permission, by Daddy, to go and camp on an island. Once again they meet supposed enemies who have a prior claim to it, but who soon turn into allies. But there are also significant differences. These waters are tidal, representing the real world they discovered aboard the *Goblin* in

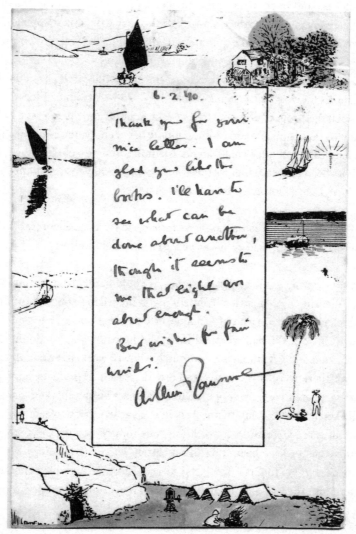

6. 2. 40.

Thank you for your nice letter. I am glad you like the books. I'll have to see what can be done about another, though it seems to me that eight are about enough.
Best wishes for fair winds.

Arthur Ransome

Arthur Ransome's postcard, found inside a first edition of *Secret Water*

the North Sea, and in contrast to the enclosed, secure 'Lake in the North'. The Swallows are given a real, grown-up task to do, surveying and mapping not just their own island but the whole archipelago, and calling for real, grown-up skills. And they have to care for a younger sibling, Bridget, and a kitten.

If Ransome had indeed wanted to bring the series full-circle, he could hardly have made a better job of it. Nancy and Peggy are re-introduced for a farewell turn, though their role of potential foe is neatly split off and given to the Eels (notice, though, the emphasis laid on the rapport between Nancy and Daisy). That this is what he did intend, or half-intend, is emphasised by a circle—the eel symbol, with its head looped under its tail—and, paradoxically, its exact opposite—a straight line. Take a look at the book's final sentence.

> The explorers, crowded aboard her, looked astern and saw the islands of the Secret
> Archipelago merge once more into an unbroken line on the horizon.

As a way of drawing a line under the series, it could hardly have been more emphatic or elegant. And this slow-fade ending is in striking contrast to his usual style, which is to finish on a bit of dialogue, often a question.

So why, if he really had wrapped it up, did he carry on? No doubt the fact that he enjoyed doing it, and it was a profitable line of work, had something to do with it, but there were also creative and artistic reasons. He might have got the Swallows to where they were supposed to go (and it's been remarked that they do not really seem to be playing themselves in the subsequent books in which they appear), but there were still a lot of loose ends to be tidied up. As a storyteller, Ransome seems to have been a bit like a carpet-weaver (an analogy that might have appealed to his folk-tale interests) forever introducing a new element into the pattern and then finding he had to create an ever-bigger carpet in order to achieve the proper symmetry.

Seen in this light, the eight books made a very unsatisfactory series. There were those Callums for a start. They had wandered into *Winter Holiday*, and seemed too good to let go. Ransome often spoke of the characters taking over, and Dick and Dot, in their unassuming way, had done just that, perhaps because they were, even more than any of the other characters, reflections of Ransome himself.

They also, as has been pointed out, gave the young readers characters with whom they could identify: ordinary children admitted, in the exquisitely-paced opening chapters of *Winter Holiday*, to the charmed circle of the lake-dwellers.

They deserved at least one more book to themselves, and ended up with two. The first, *The Big Six*, provided a return to the Broads, and another platform for Joe, Bill and Pete, for whom Ransome had developed considerable affection. It also gave him a chance to dabble in the detective-story genre, of which he was fond—he used to review batches of detective books for the *Observer*. *The Big Six*, as Dorothea is, oddly, allowed to point out in an isolated paragraph on the title page, is an allusion to the 'Big Five'—'the greatest detectives in the world. They sit in their cubby-holes in Scotland Yard and solve one mystery after another.' Dorothea is obviously, like Ransome, a connoisseur of crime fiction, but the Big Five were indeed real. The name was journalistic shorthand for the detective chief superintendedents of the four Metropolitan Police districts of London, plus the head of the CID.

The other D's book, *The Picts and the Martyrs*, reflects another of Ransome's tastes—for social comedy, never too far away when Dorothea's involved. Ransome was a great fan of P. G. Wodehouse, and even named not one but two of his later boats after a Wodehouse character, Lottie Blossom. *The Picts and the Martyrs* also gave Nancy the leading role she'd no doubt stormed into Ransome's study and demanded, in a convoluted comedy of concealment and subterfuge that precisely suited her talents (and compensated her for being left out of *We Didn't Mean to Go to Sea*).

Missee Lee is another fantasy—a sort of *Peter Duck* in the South China Seas (and sadly without Peter Duck himself)—which also served to provide a stage for Ransome's Chinese experiences.

It's arguable that while each of these has its own merits, they add little to the coherence of the series—but then if you look at the foregoing eight, there is often a battle going on between coherence and disparity. (Where would *Coot Club* fit into this scheme of things for example?). There is in fact little evidence that Ransome set out with a scheme, or regarded himself as beholden to completing a pattern. Rather, he seems to have worked in quite the opposite way, finishing one book and wondering where the next one was coming from. And yet, perhaps subconsciously, he always seems to have had an ear for that inner balance and elegance which define the books as a series, rather than just twelve different tales about the same cast of characters. And in *Great Northern*, he brings the whole thing to a close with a grand flourish, bringing together all the main characters, the Swallows, the Amazons, the D's and Uncle Jim, and setting the climax on a lake, within an island, within a sea.

Of all the books, only two, *Great Northern* and *Secret Water*, have this quality of consciously delivering closure. Perhaps Ransome did intend to stop with *Secret Water*. We might be grateful that he didn't, but we should pause to admire, and enjoy, the satisfying dynamic of the shorter series within the larger.

CHAPTER SIX

Storytellers

୧୬

R ansome used to say that behind the shoulder of every storyteller is another storyteller, and behind him, another, as far back as we can see. The remark reached me, appropriately enough orally, from the lips of another fine storyteller, Hugh Lupton, Ransome's nephew, part of whose stock-in-trade are Ransome's *Old Peter's Russian Tales*. Hugh, as part of his set-up for telling one of Ransome's Russian stories, describes Ransome as standing behind his shoulder, and behind Ransome, the first, or the last, in a succession of old Russian talespinners.

This idea of a chain of storytellers, passing tales down through the ages, modifying and improving or adapting them as they went, had a particular appeal to Ransome, who loved the idea that there was such a community—or such a role in the wider, more general community—and that he was part of it.

For Ransome, the most obvious predecessor is Stevenson. Ransome takes the key elements of *Treasure Island* and reworks them on a more domestic, enclosed, safe scale, set on a lake, with dinghies, and a small island that a boy can swim right round before lunch. And then, magically, he does it again, in *Peter Duck*, transmuting these elements, now from his own story, but this time projected through the imaginations of the children themselves back onto the 'real' world—real seas, and a real or realistic Caribbean island, and 'real' pirates—really nasty, at any rate, and most inspired of all, held together by the most definitively imaginary character, Titty's 'friend' Peter Duck, being the most real of the lot of them—a real seaman from a real ship, the clipper *Thermopylae*—and based on Ransome's old sailing companion from his *Racundra* days, the 'Ancient Mariner' Carl Sehmel.

For *We Didn't Mean to Go to Sea*, however, he drew for inspiration on another, and comparatively exclusive, group of authors. The seafaring community has its own tales and tellers, and the purpose of this chapter is to introduce some of the narrators who were clustered around Ransome at his desk when he was writing

71

it—or more probably sharing, in spirit, the cockpit of the *Nancy Blackett* with him, as he mused on the story and figured it out.

They are a very different crew from the earlier books' Stevenson and Defoe, or even from Nansen, whose guest appearance so charmingly informs *Winter Holiday*. They are all of them practical yachtsmen whose experience informs their writings about the sea and whose work, and in many cases lives and voyages, Ransome greatly admired. Most of them were subsequently to have their work re-published in the *Mariner's Library*, set up by Rupert Hart-Davis, and which Ransome helped edit, and for some titles wrote introductions. They crop up, usually incognito, in the pages of *We Didn't Mean to Go to Sea* and give it the richness and depth that make it the great work that it is.

When Jim Brading says 'Only one motto for the *Goblin*. When in doubt keep clear of shoals... Get out to sea and stay there,' he is in effect repeating the advice of R. T. McMullen, of whose *Down Channel*, published in 1869, Ransome wrote 'No man who has read this book ever forgets it.'

Ransome himself first read it in Finland, at the Nylands Yacht Club in Helsingfors where, as he records in *Racundra's First Cruise*, he found the library had 'a really wonderful collection of sailing-books from all the countries of the world'. 'After dinner,' he writes in *Racundra*, 'I.. went into the Club library and... for the first time, settled down to read McMullen. Few books on sailing fail to quote McMullen, but his own book is rare, and I was glad enough to read, out here, on a Finnish island, the story of *Orion*'s return from France... It was after midnight before I put the book back on its shelf and, dropping over the pierhead into the dinghy, threaded my way in the dark through the little fleet to *Racundra*'s gleaming portholes.'

Richard Tyrrell McMullen was one of the first of the Corinthian sailors (i.e., those who believed in doing it themselves, often in small boats, rather than, as owners, sitting on the after-deck with a drink while paid hands actually sailed the boat). According to Ransome, in his 'biographical foreword' to the *Mariner's Library* edition of *Down Channel*, 'He set himself a much higher standard of efficiency in amateur sailing than had ever been set before.' And he insisted that the sea was far less dangerous than the land in a blow. 'If it looks like blowing hard on shore, get in somewhere in good time or else give the land a very wide berth,' was the advice which Ransome quotes him as giving to Claud Worth. He was, comments Ransome, 'The first to insist that the danger most to be apprehended by skippers of all sailing vessels was (after screw steamers) not water but land.'

It's advice which John takes instinctively to heart, once the *Goblin* has drifted out to sea. 'Remenber what Jim said about the man who lost his boat,' he tells Susan, 'When in doubt keep clear of shoals. Get out to sea and stay there. If he were on board he'd be doing it now... we're at sea now, and we can't get back in the fog.'

Curiously, E. E. Middleton, for whose *The Cruise of the Kate* Ransome also provided an admiring foreword, took at first sight the opposite approach to McMullen. He liked to sleep in a bed, so his single-handed round-Britain cruise is punctuated by frequent landfalls. One leg, after leaving Lyme Regis at 3am, with several hours of being becalmed, brings him to Torquay in the late afternoon. He writes: 'I ate nothing throughout the day but a little bread, and breakfasted at the Imperial Hotel at the late hour of 6.30pm.' It's not a bad joke, and Ransome gets full value out of it when he borrows it for Jim Brading.

> 'And then...' he yawned and rubbed his eyes... 'I'll see what the Butt can do me by way of breakfast...'
>
> 'Breakfast!' Susan, Titty and Roger all exclaimed together. 'But it's nearly seven o'clock. Haven't you had anything to eat all day?'

Ransome's admiration of Middleton seems based on his modesty of aspiration and achievement, which seems to strike a chord with Ransome's own make-up. That and 'a happy and suitable eccentricity of person,' in which Ransome also perceives a fellow-spirit.

It might seem odd to describe a circumnavigation of Britain as 'modest', particularly when this was the first single-handed such voyage, but that is the word Ransome chooses, though he also describes it as 'remarkable'. Breaking the voyage down into bite-size chunks might seem easy, but it does mean the yachtsman is forever coping with 'rocks, sands, tide-races and treacherous shallows', which he would avoid were he to follow McMullen's example and put out to sea and stay there.

It is this self-imposed difficulty that Ransome admires, even though it is born of ignorance—Middleton has no experience of cruising in small craft, or even of being in control of a boat, except for a few lessons in Southampton Water on a hired cutter. When he sets off, he has failed to realise that he would need navigation lights after dark. He orders some to be picked up at Southampton, having sailed there from the Thames without, but neglects to fit boards to keep them showing as they should, and simply hangs them in the rigging. There they swing and revolve—'an infuriating puzzle to vessels unfortunate enough to sight them,' comments Ransome. He adds: 'The first single-handed navigation of England was the work of a novice, and of one who in writing his account of it was still not always conscious that he was telling a cautionary tale.'

But if E. E. Middleton shares some affinity with Ransome as he really was—never throughout his life a particularly venturesome yachtsman—then E. F. Knight, the exuberant adventurer, is Captain Flint in his dreams. (Captain Flint/Uncle Jim is perceived by the children in the books as being the fount of all adult wisdom, particularly in things to do with sailing, but Ransome is careful to reveal his imperfections and limitations. His explorations abroad are generally unsuccessful, and in *Peter Duck* he is seen deferring to the greater experience and wisdom of Mr Duck, much as Ransome himself did, in *Racundra*, to Carl Sehmel, the Ancient Mariner.)

Knight's manual on sailing is very much a touchstone in the twelve books. When the *Goblin* is anchored on Felixstowe Shelf waiting for Jim and the fog comes down, 'John went down into the cabin and took Knight's *Sailing* from the bookshelf. He looked up the page about signals in fog.'

And in *The Picts and the Martyrs*, when Dick and Dot have met up on the train going to the lake, in Chapter 2, 'Dick had opened his suitcase and taken out a thin blue book, *Sailing*, by E. F. Knight, on which he meant to put in some hard work during the journey.' Knight becomes Dick's constant companion, as they take delivery of, and then learn to sail, the *Scarab*.

But it's not Knight's thin blue manual, a copy of which now resides on *Nancy*'s bookshelf, that makes its presence most felt in *We Didn't Mean to Go to Sea*. Rather, it's his *The Falcon on the Baltic*, an account of sailing a converted ship's lifeboat from Hammersmith to Copenhagen, which Ransome described, in a let-

ter to Rupert Hart-Davis, as 'a real beauty of a book, from the sailing point of
view, and from the merely human... I read it at least once a year.'

And, as he says in his introduction to the *Mariner's Library* edition, 'Grown-
up people (if those who love sailing ever grow up, which I doubt) are like children
in taking particular pleasure in stories that tell of adventures that might happen,
with luck, to themselves.' Part of the *Falcon*'s voyage takes her from Harwich
harbour to Holland (Rotterdam, actually) so perhaps it's only to be expected that
aspects of her adventures also happen to the *Goblin*.

Consider this passage:

> The wind gradually freshened as the day advanced, and I observed that the aneroid
> in the cabin was steadily falling. At midday I brought up my sextant to shoot the
> sun and found that we were exactly on our course. The wind still freshened and
> we were rushing through the water faster than ever. 'I don't like the sky now,' said
> Wright; 'It looks very wild. It will blow to-night.'
>
> 'Yes, we must carry on as much as we can, and try to get hold of the land be-
> fore dark.'
>
> 'It's a pity we didn't sail last night after all. We should have been in Rotterdam
> by now,' remarked Wright. I had been thinking the same thing to myself, but as we
> were in the middle of the North Sea by this time, it was clear that we must run on,
> there could be no turning back now. A steep, high sea was following us, but the
> boat behaved splendidly.

Different boat, different crew, different voyage, but the same sense, vividly conveyed, of being thrust on by the wind.

> 'It was blowing harder now, and the *Goblin* was racing through the fog, heaving
> high on the top of a sea and dropping into a trough, only to be heaved high again as
> another rose under her.'

Like Knight, John's instinct is to run on, before the wind, and he's proved correct
when he is prevailed upon by Susan to try turning back. This is when the *Goblin*
ships a lot of water, and Roger looks down into the cabin and notices a book float-

ing about. A few pages later, its identity is revealed.

> Roger caught Knight on *Sailing*, that John had not put away. He grabbed it out of
> the water, and, just in time, was stopped from pushing it in among the dry books.
> 'Put it in the sink,' said Titty, 'to let it drain.'

Or this, from Knight:

> It was about this time that we came upon a fleet of Dutch fishermen, great tubby
> craft with leeboards, which were rolling in a comfortable, lazy way that gave one
> the impression of their being quite safe, and very much at home in this sort of
> water.

The *Goblin* also meets some fishing boats. 'Most of them haven't got pointed
bows at all... round like apples... I do believe they're Dutch. ...Gosh how they
roll!' There are 'a dozen or so of them, rolling heavily, plunging along, every now
and then taking a sea, thump, on their bluff bows with a sudden explosion of white
spray.'... 'They've got leeboards,' said Roger, 'like barges, but they're not a bit
like them in other ways.' The 'big, varnished boats, their oaken topsides shining
in the sun' cross *Goblin*'s wake... 'and on all the fishing boats, arms were flung up
and a cheer came over the water for the little English boat that has come so far.'
   The *Falcon* also exchanges greetings with the fishing-boats.

> We passed close to some of these boats and hailed the men, asking them how far
> off land we were. I don't know whether they understood us, but they shrieked back
> replies which we certainly could not understand, so we ran on eastwards, hoping
> soon to find the coast.

The *Falcon*, unlike the *Goblin*, does not rescue a shipwrecked kitten, but both vessels encounter steamers, and pass a light-ship in the night. And then there are the
pilots.
   'It is against my principles to employ a pilot on a small yacht,' declares Knight.
But they are tired, the weather is bad and they are among dangerous shoals, so

they signal for one anyway. 'He threw into the cabin that oilskin bundle which invariably represents a pilot's luggage, shook hands with me and inquired where I wanted to go to. 'Hellevoetsluis,' I replied. 'Right, captain, I will take you there, and I shan't be long about it with this wind.''

And in *We Didn't Mean to Go to Sea*:

> A round bundle of oilskin landed in the cockpit with a thud. Big hairy hands, with mottlings of blue under the hair, grasped the coaming. There was a shout in a foreign language. The rowing boat drifted astern. A broad, blue-clothed, red-face man scrambled into the cockpit... 'Good day, mynheer,' said the pilot, reaching for the tiller, 'You want me to take you into Flushing?'

Both pilots, who curiously seem to speak the same kind of slightly fractured English, are complimentary about the respective boats. 'Capital boat to run before the sea this, captain,' says Knight's. 'Little boat, but ver' good,' says Ransome's.

And the local people are equally impressed. Knight, having visited the harbour office 'returned to my yacht and found a great many people, of all ranks, ages and sexes, gazing at us from the quay, and discussing us in the curiously deliberate and unexcitable Dutch fashion. One who spoke English explained to me the sentiments of his fellows. 'These Holland people,' he said, 'think your boat too little to cross the North Sea. They not like to be passengers of you, not at all, by Jove.''

Likewise, the crew of the *Goblin*, returning from their meal with Daddy, find 'a crowd of children on the grass between the street and the water,' and the pilot talking to them. ''Well, Capten,' said the pilot to John. 'These boys and girls dey not believe you bring your ship across de Nord See. Hey? But I tell dem.''

Perhaps it was as well Ransome was able to draw on Knight's experiences. His own voyage from Harwich to Flushing in *Nancy Blackett* by way of research for the book was almost entirely uneventful, and he—like Knight in normal times—disdained to take a pilot, although he subsequently made the acquaintance of one, pilot de Smit, in Flushing.

Ransome is not the only respected author to borrow from Knight. Erskine Childers, in *The Riddle of the Sands*, has Davies describing the *Dulcibella*'s voyage to the Frisian Islands. Like Knight, he came up through the Dutch canals. And, exactly like Knight, he suffered persecution at the hands of small boys—'the most troublesome urchins of all Europe,' according to Knight, who hurled stones and even bricks at his boat. Davies likewise complains: 'Heavens! Shall I ever forget those boys! A perfect murrain of them infests Holland; they seem to have nothing in the world to do but throw stones and mud at foreign yachts.' A little later, Davies explicitly invokes Knight: 'I decided to go straight for the Baltic. I always had an idea of getting there, as Knight did in the *Falcon*.' And the book itself is on *Dulcibella*'s bookshelf, along with McMullen's *Down Channel* and Cowper's *Sailing Tours*. There's a pilot, too, this time on the Schlei Fjord in the Baltic, who marvels at 'so little a ship'.

But Childers, too, like the wise men, or the godmothers (the good ones) in *Sleeping Beauty*, has a gift for Ransome's fledgling story. Here is Carruthers, the narrator:

> A blunder of mine, when I went to the winch to get up the anchor, settled the question. Thirty of our forty fathoms of chain were out. Confused by the motion and a blinding sleet-shower that had come on, and forgetting the tremendous strain on the cable, I cast the slack off the bitts and left it loose. There was only one turn of the chain round the drum, enough in ordinary weather to prevent it running out. But now my first heave on the winch-lever started it slipping, and in an instant it was whizzing out of the hawse-pipe and overboard. I tried to stop it with my foot, stumbled at a heavy plunge of the yacht, heard something snap below and saw the last of it disappear.

Childers is more economical; Ransome's use of a similar incident is more atmospheric and dramatic—appropriately because it forms a major turning-point in the development of the narrative.

> There was a rattle and roar as the loose chain he had hauled up on deck came flying out over the fairlead close to the bowsprit. More chain came pouring up out of the hawse-pipe and went to join the rest.

John tries to stamp on the chain to stop it, but is instantly unbalanced by it:

> He had no time to do another thing before he saw the end of the chain come up out
> of the chain-pipe and fly over the bows with a bit of frayed rope flying after it.

In the *Riddle*, it's a comparatively minor incident, affecting merely their choice of
direction, and of little concern to the capable, laconic Davies:

> 'Doesn't matter,' he said; 'anchor's buoyed. We'll come back tomorrow and get
> it. Can't now. Should have had to slip it anyhow; wind and sea too strong. We'll
> try for Bensersiel. Can't trust to a warp and kedge out here.'

For John, it's a major catastrophe, and a personal failure:

> 'It's all gone,' he panted. 'All his chain and his anchor. I've let it all go overboard.'

And then, of course, the even worse realization:

> 'John,' cried Susan. 'We're adrift.'

It's always been a matter of regret to me that Ransome did not write one of his
introductions for the Mariner's Library edition of The Riddle of the Sands. That
he had read the book is obvious—also that he admired it. He once described it as
'the best yachting story ever written,' and added 'I never knew anybody who was
content to read it only once'. It's mentioned in Winter Holiday as one of the books
on the shelves of Captain Flint's houseboat (though Dorothea decides that it 'did
not seem her sort of book').

Incidentally, it's by no means impossible that Ransome and Childers would
have met each other. *The Riddle of the Sands* came out in 1903 when Ransome,
then aged nineteen, had already moved to London. Within a year he had moved
to Chelsea, where Childers also lived. It seems unlikely that their respective literary circles would not have overlapped at some point, though whether the callow
youth of twenty and the newly-married author fourteen years his senior would

have had much in common is debatable. Still it would have been interesting to know a bit more about Ransome's thoughts on the book and its author. Both Ransome, in Russia, and Childers, in Ireland, got mixed up in revolutionary politics. Both of them used their own boats in their books. Childers' *Vixen*, the original of the *Dulcibella*, sadly rotted away in Lymington—she was almost beyond saving when Ransome would have passed by on his 1935 delivery voyage in *Nancy*—and was finally broken up in 1948.

And then there's Maurice Griffiths. It's been suggested (by Roger Wardale in *Ransome at Sea*) that the germ of the plot of *We Didn't Mean to Go to Sea* is to be found in Griffiths' *The Magic of the Swatchways*.

This renowned volume of autobiographical East Coast sailing anecdotes was published in 1932. The passage in question comes from the chapter entitled 'With *Juanita* to the 'Other Side'', which begins thus:

> The mournful tolling of the bell-buoy at the mouth of the harbour, a spasmodic, cacophonous din as the iron cage rose and fell on the uneasy swell that gurgled past its weedy sides, reflected the feeling of depression which had descended upon me. The ebb-tide, pouring in a vast oily stream out of Harwich Harbour, carried *Juanita* with it, while her sails flapped aimlessly in the calm evening air, and as we drifted out past Landguard Point into the well-named Rolling Ground, I sat with the lifeless tiller in one hand and thought how foolish it was to start on a long passage across the North Sea in a flat calm with a yacht that has no engine...

Seemingly it's all there: right place, the significance of the buoy (which is probably the Beach End), the drifting, engineless yacht. Except that it isn't, really. The yacht, which is owned by Griffiths' wife, known as 'Peter' is intentionally without an engine. The drift, too, is intentional, or at least the passage which it initiates is, a holiday voyage across 'a hundred miles of treacherous sea' to, as it happens, Flushing—though they have a considerably harder time of it than the *Goblin*, and divert to Ostend instead.

Perhaps it formed part of the mix of memories and references out of which Ransome forged the plot of *We Didn't Mean to Go to Sea*. He certainly owned the book—his 1932 edition is now in the Fullerton Library in America, with others from his library. However, Harwich Harbour was very much Ransome's own territory. He could see much of it from the window of his study at Broke Farm, Levington, and he sailed constantly out of, into and around it in *Nancy*. He knew its tides, its channels and its buoys. None of which, of course, actually prevents him from nurturing and turning to good use a germ of an idea picked up from reading Maurice Griffiths.

But if he did, then I sense he did so subconsciously, and without the sense of *hommage* with which I imagine him gleefully and deliberately importing elements from his literary heroes. In fact, I'd go so far as to perceive that there may have been a coolness between Ransome and Griffiths. There is no conclusive evidence to support this, but it seems strange that the two writers seem to have made little effort to cultivate each other's acquaintance, when they doubtless had every opportunity to do so—Griffiths designed *Lapwing*, the boat belonging to Ransome's great friend Colonel Busk, which appears in *Secret Water* under its own name as the 'mission ship'. It's also perhaps significant that Ransome never contributed to *Yachting Monthly*, which Griffiths edited for 40 years from 1927 to 1967.

Possibly the matter of the strangely-similar illustrations has some bearing on things. Ransome's depiction of the *Goblin* in 'All but O.B.' is striking for its unusual angle of view—overhead and off the starboard bow—but is also strikingly similar to a drawing by Griffiths in his *Ten Small Yachts*, published in 1933. We can be sure Ransome had seen it, for he reviewed the book for the *Manchester Guardian* (favourably enough, though he—Ransome!—describes Griffiths as 'dreadfully fickle' for his continual shifting of his flag).

Straight poaching seems the only available explanation, other than extreme absent-mindendness. In later years, though, Griffiths was very gracious about it. In correspondence with Dennis Bird, who like most of Ransome's sailing fans was also a fan of Griffiths, he shrugged-off the similarity in the drawings: 'Both show yachts in much the same position on a breezy day running before a following sea. Beyond that, I wouldn't claim that Ransome deliberately copied the *Afrin* sketch…If Ransome's does indeed seem to be a copy of mine, I can only say that imitation is the sincerest form of flattery.' He did however take the opportunity to criticise Ransome's grasp of technical detail. '…the forceful bow-wave any yacht thrusts before her in the conditions shown is completely absent from the bow of

Goblin. The jibsheet looks almost close-hauled, and the mainsheet doesn't appear to be in the running position.'

Asked about his relationship with Ransome himself, he diplomatically replied:

> Strangely enough, although I enjoyed most of Ransome's books, and knew the yachts he owned, I have always been sorry that I hardly knew him. We only met during weekends afloat, on Pin Mill hard or elsewhere along the coast. I knew Colonel Busk of course, having as you say designed *Lapwing* for him and his family.

Ransome was also happy to plunder his own back-catalogue for material which would enrich the Swallows' experience. Everybody remembers the arrival of the jolly Dutch pilot:

> A broad, blue-clothed, red-faced man scrambled into the cockpit... 'Good day, mynheer, you want me to take you into Flushing?'

And, once *Goblin*'s tied up, banging on her hatch and shouting, 'NOW, CAPTEN!'. Like most Ransome fans, I read *We Didn't Mean to Go to Sea* long before I read *Racundra's First Cruise*—where I was surprised to find this:

> There was a splash of a boat in the water, a bobbing lantern appearing and disappearing in the waves, and a large Finnish pilot tumbled on board with: 'Where do you want to go? ... Nylands Club? ... Right. Keep Grohara light so. Now, Captain...'

Here's John, sailing the *Goblin*, alone at night, counting the seconds between the flashes from the lightship to keep awake:

> Whatever happened, he simply must not go to sleep. If only he could sing he could keep awake. But he could not sing because of waking Susan. Suddenly he started. A sail was clapping like thunder. The wind was blowing not from behind him but into his face. The tiller was kicking this way and that and the *Goblin* was plunging up and down like a mad thing. Two bright flashes shone not on the starboard bow

but somewhere away to port.

'John! John! What's happened?' Susan had waked in terror.

'I fell asleep,' he shouted into the wind.

And here's Ransome, in *Racundra*, on what he describes as 'a wild, but in a curious way, rather enjoyable night.'

> I suppose everybody who has spent long hours at the tiller of a little boat has done the same. But, I admit, I was startled the first time I woke to find myself in the well of *Racundra*, holding a kicking tiller, with the dark in my eyes, and a great wind in my face.

He pinches himself to keep awake—John gets Susan to do it for him, and eventually hands over the tiller to her.

Racundra has had to take in her mainsail after the gaff jaws had broken, and is 'careering through steep seas in a pitch-dark night with no sidelights and a binnacle lamp that would not burn.' Ransome has already decided against making for the harbour mouth and dropping anchor there.

> I knew the place well from other years, and so knew that the depth was far too great to give us a chance of doing anything but lose an anchor, and if we got anywhere near the shore, unless actually in the harbour mouth, we should infallibly go on a rock.

Instead, he elects to head out to sea, and carry on till morning. This is the same night, by the way, that the cook (Evgenia) asks if they are to be drowned, or whether she should keep one of the flasks of coffee till tomorrow.

'On the face of it,' writes Ransome, 'misery. Yet there was no misery about it. While in that narrow bay, I was very much afraid, but here in the open sea, things were better. Besides, we were doing the thing which I had myself urged as the right thing to do.' Just like John, who experiences 'a serious kind of joy,' and 'a little ashamedly admitted to himself that he was happy', so Ransome records, 'I had the joy of possession'. Unlike John, he does sing, yelling *Spanish Ladies* among others at the top of his voice. Like John, eventually he falls asleep.

But for both Ransome and John, the arrival of dawn is greeted as a sort of blessing on their endeavours.

'And then suddenly, with a relief which let me know how great the strain had been, I knew that the eastern sky was distinguishable from the sea,' writes Ransome in *Racundra*. 'Day was coming at last and with day the possibility of doing more than holding our own… Day came, or the light before the day, and I found exultantly that I was now not sleepy at all. We had done much better than I had expected in the dark… Everything was hope.'

And aboard the *Goblin*:

> Jolly cold it was, but who cared? Dawn was coming. Susan was all right again. The wind had gone down. The sea wasn't half as bad as it had been. And the *Goblin* was still afloat, swinging comfortably along just as if she had not found out that Jim Brading was not at the tiller. John's hands might be a bit cold, but there was a pleasant glow in his inside at the thought of how much worse things might have been.

There seems to be much more going on here than the recycling of a few remembered incidents to thicken the authenticity of the tale. John's emotions are Ransome's on *Racundra*, and in transferring them to a character on the verge of manhood, Ransome is perhaps reliving and re-examining a rite of passage in his own sailing life. He was, it has to be said, a very much better writer about sailing than he was a sailor. He was deeply stirred by the sea, and man's relationship with it, and he took very seriously the wisdom of McMullen and Knight, along with the whole ritual attached to sailing a boat, which he loved to insert, to very good effect, into his stories. In fact, one might say that if his politics were fishing, as he once claimed, then his religion was sailing and his writing about it often approached the status of liturgy.

But that said, of offshore sailing he did relatively little. That night in *Racundra*, and his delivery trip from Poole with *Nancy Blackett* represent the most extreme conditions he encountered. Otherwise his level was gentle coastal cruising, and not a lot of it. Perhaps it was because he came relatively late in life to sailing in the coastal waters of England that his horizons remained relatively limited. And perhaps that was why he invested John, always in the books the capable strong boy which he himself had never been, with the hopes and dreams which he had never quite managed to fulfill for himself. 'Years and years hence, when he was grown up he would have a ship of his own , and sail her into wider seas than this.'

Racundra was the lived experience, directly described. *We Didn't Mean to Go to Sea* is the result of the process of sifting and sorting it, along with the experience of others, into literature. In accomplishing it, Ransome in effect became one with that company of storytellers hovering at his shoulder.

Saturday to Saturday

by Arthur Ransome
From the Cruising Association *Bulletin*, December 1937

N*ancy Blackett* is a 7-ton bm. cutter, wl.l. 26.5, b.8.2, d.5. Engine: Handy Billy. Dinghy (towed throughout): *Queen Mary*, a first cousin of *Ianthe*'s *Wee Pup*. Crew: her owner and Rouse, who was at school with me full forty years ago. We had only one week to spare from work. Rouse joined at Pin Mill on the evening of Whit-Friday, and we dropped down the river and anchored above Felixstowe dock.

Saturday, May 15. We woke to a cold dull morning with fresh North Easterly wind, and spent some time getting ready for sea. Up anchor at 10.10, setting jib and reefed mainsail. The flood had begun as we left Beach End buoy at 10.30. Visibility was not too good. By 12.30 we were half way through the Spitway, going along at a comfortable wallop and rejoicing that we were not aboard a ML which passed us, rolling gaily. We passed the Maplin Spit buoy at 2.15. We were old enough to have made no plans, and were debating whether or no to make an easy first day of it by going to Queenborough when, after getting to a good strategic position by the Oaze, the sight of the Girdler and the realization that we should just be able to lay our course to the E. Tongue made it seem a crime not to push on for Dover or Ramsgate. So we bucketed along, close-hauled, by Pan Sand, N. Tongue and E. Tongue buoys, wind and sea increasing, but not enough to worry *Nancy*, who was asking no more than a finger's pressure on the tiller.

We made the NE Spit towards dusk. There was a good deal of traffic, and twice we had to show a light from the cockpit to steamers coming up astern. We had a grand sail past Ramsgate's blazing front, and I was considering making a night of it and going right on when I heard a slight rattle forward and found that the rigging screws of the starboard shrouds had all but unscrewed themselves. I put this right as well as I could in the dark, and then, as it was blowing pretty hard and gusty and inclined to rain, decided to go into Dover and wire them properly in daylight. At 10.50 pm (12 hours and 20 minutes out from Harwich) we passed through the eastern entrance with Billy ticking over ready to do his job when wanted. We took in sail in the outer harbour, not without a bit of trouble. The jib would not roll up, and the blocks were looking for a chance to box somebody's ears. Then with all sails on deck and Billy going slow we groped for the Submarine Basin, which neither of us had entered before. I half expected to find it a sardine tin, close packed with submarines instead of sardines, but found it a fine little place with plenty of room, though in the dark and the rain it was hard to see just how much room there was. Rouse went forward to play with the anchor.

I could not see what he was doing and a slight misunderstanding resulted in our being blown back too near the entrance before the anchor went down. He yanked it off the bottom again, and when I put Billy in gear to get back to our chosen spot, the propeller wound up *Queen Mary*'s painter and cut her adrift. Luckily she drifted into a patch of light by the entrance, and Billy, in spite of adornments, gave enough steerage way to let me steam round and catch *QM* with the long boat hook. Rouse, meanwhile, was wondering what was happening, as he could no more see what I was doing than I could see what was engaging him. This time he had all ready to let go on the instant, and in a few minutes the anchor was down, *QM* was on a new painter, the Bogie stove was alight, and supper was well under way. I was an ass not to have hauled the dinghy up short before going into the Submarine Basin when I was fully occupied with lead and tiller.

May 16. Bright, clear, cold day, with gentle NE wind.

We could see the propeller looking like Medusa's hellish mop. A man sailing a pretty little Harrison Butler passed close by and told us where we could put her on the hard to clear it. We debated this. It would have meant the loss of a whole day. We decided to try something else first. Rouse, who is luckily of light displacement, knelt, stripped to the waist in *QM*, tied under *Nancy*'s transom. I took my colossal weight out on the bowsprit end to help cock up the stern of the ship. Rouse, plunging his arm to the shoulder, carved away at the tangled rope till he had a free end to pull on. Then he sang out to me to come and turn the engine over to unwind it. A short bit would come away, and I would then resume my place to smoke a pipe in comfort on the bowsprit, while he went to work again with his knife till he had freed another end. Then more unwinding, another scrap of rope removed, and me once more the idle lounger on the bowsprit and he once more the gallant diver. This went on until, with chattering teeth, Rouse announced that the propeller was clear. I poured neat rum into him and am happy to say that he suffered no ill effects. A solid beef steak pudding luncheon may have helped.

HWD was at 4.28 pm BST. We cleared Dover East Entrance at 4.30, with the wind NE by E. Full sail. The tide was still pouring East. We kept Billy on light duty till 5.20 when we shut him off, satisfied that the propeller had not been damaged either by growing a mop or by having it shaved. At 7.45 we had Folkestone abeam and laid a course for Dungeness. At 9.30 Rouse went below for a sleep, making me promise to call him at midnight. I was a selfish pig and didn't, but had a grand time at the tiller. A fine night and a good wind, though a bit near jibing point, steamers as usual thick as slugs after dark, though we had seen few before, *Nancy* smoking along, her wash and bow wave alight with phosphorescence, and *Queen Mary* planing after her in a bath of green fire. 11.39 pm Dungeness lights in line.

May 17. 3.30 am, Rouse, expostulating at not having been called, came up and took over. I had filled two thermos flasks with hot soup before leaving Dover, and we shared one of them (pea) just as the day was opening. I went down for a sleep. 6.15. passing the Royal Sovereign, we shared the second flask, this time tomato. I went under again. At 8 am Beachy Head was abeam. From 8.30 to 9.30 we breakfasted, milk, cornflakes, tea and scrambled eggs (my star turn). At 9.15, very disgusted with myself. I dug out the log and put it over, reading zero. I had meant to do this at the Royal Sovereign. Too sleepy, I suppose, but a poor excuse. We had to estimate backwards.

We now began to see things, Nab Tower away to port, a dim hint of the Wight, forts and moored ships of war ahead, and we had a fine burst home as dusk fell, calling on Billy to help us over the tide pouring out from Spithead. At 10.30 pm we were forcing our way into Portsmouth. Picket boats and what-nots of horrible speed were dashing out, and a steamer, like ourselves, was struggling in over the tide. We kept along the Eastern side of the harbour, past the docks, and groped our way into the Porchester [sic] channel, where, when I could no longer see the booms against the sky, we anchored for the night.

May 18. We slept very late, and woke to see Porchester Castle, where I wanted to anchor, a little way ahead. We were a little disturbed by a large red notice on a boom at the side of the channel. Rouse, very properly, wanted to row over and see what it said. I, less dutiful, said 'Better not'. I got the glasses on it and could read '£50.' I thought better not know any more, so that we could plead that we had come in in the dark and perhaps be let off some of our £50. But presently a rattle of rifle fire told us all about it. Rouse got the anchor up in record time and we motored up the channel, mooring under the lovely old castle astern of other small vessels.

We tidied up, lunched, put on our pretties, and went shopping in Portsmouth, to get a new mainsheet, food and a book of directions for the use of our new Pentacon cooking pot, which, so far, had been an idle passenger. We got a lovely mainsheet and then separated, agreeing to meet at an inn, when, if Rouse had got the sailing directions for the Pentacon, I was to buy a steak and see what could he done with it. Rouse walked all over Portsmouth and succeeded in getting an advertisement of the Pentacon with enough explanations on it to give me a chance of getting the instrument to work. I reached the inn at seven with a kitbag full of fruit, bread, and other things, and after a glance at the advertisement rushed out to find a butcher. It was after closing time, but in the end I was directed to a shop where the butcher lived over his work. I knocked at the door and found that the butcher had gone out for the evening. His wife, however, had a kind heart and said they had a friend there who knew something about butching. This friend and I invaded the butcher's refrigerator. He was on the point of giving me one or two nice little parcels addressed to various Portsmouth ladies, but thought better of it... 'You never know if they're one of them nasty ones...' and I thought privately that even a nice one might turn a bit nasty if she found her special steak had been handed out to somebody else. In the end we found a large joint, out of the middle of which the butcher's friend cut me a lovely chunk, making the joint look rather funny. He looked at it sadly and then admitted that he wasn't a butcher really, and had never cut meat before. His business, I gathered, had been at the till. I only hope his friend the butcher was not too hard on him when he saw what he had done. I went off with my lump of beef complete with skewer, and we had a very good meal at the inn, and then back to Porchester, launched our dinghy under the castle, and so home to *Nancy* and bed.

We had learnt in Portsmouth that on the day of the Coronation Review there would be a lot of restrictions on movement, and decided that if we were to wait for the review it might mean the loss of two whole days out of our precious week, so that, with a long way to go, we had better get about our business and start home in the morning.

May 19. Started from Porchester under power at 11.25, hoisting sail under way. We spoke *Amaryllis*, anchored below us, getting ready for the review. The wind was S by E, light. A grand day though a little misty. We had a last look at the huge grey islands of the fleet moored in Spithead, and were off, passing between the Dolphins at 12.35. Full sail. Decided to keep Billy running at half throttle till we were through the Looe. At 2.25 we passed the Street buoy, and at 2.40 shut off Billy and put over the log, reading 36.5. Lovely to be back in the peace of sail only.

Rouse was at the helm while I had a long struggle with the stoves and the new Pentacon, finally packing it with steak and vegetables and letting it rip. Took it off the stove when the whistle blew, and half an hour later found really first class steak inside it. Blunt knives cut it like butter.

We had chosen Newhaven as our next 'strategic position,' and before Rouse made ready to go below for a sleep we had sighted the harbour lights, but, when already close to the harbour, we decided to get out, open Beachy Head light and carry on. I had a pleasant, long, lazy watch, steering through the dark till daybreak, when I hogged a whole thermos flask full of hot soup. Round Beachy there was a mob of steamers. Steered for the Royal Sovereign, and thence for Dungeness.

May 20. Rouse had very little wind after dawn and it was getting on for noon before we were nearing Dungeness. We were making hardly any progress, so ran in under the west side and at 12.30 pm anchored in four fathoms, bathed and lunched. At 1.20 pm we were off again, light headwind and tide against us. Started Billy. Dungeness lights in line 1.50 pm. Here we dawdled. Rouse had given *Nancy* a mackerel line in Portsmouth and was anxious to see her catch her first fish. He saw some gulls which he thought were diving after sprats, and there would have been a mutiny if we had not trailed our spinner over the spot. We shut off Billy, to give the spinner its best chance, but there was no result, and, fearing that *Nancy* was smelling the ground, I cruelly disregarded the fisherman, restarted Billy, and let him tick over to help the sails, proceeding closehauled on starboard tack, and gradually closing the land towards Hythe. Then we made a board out to sea. Billy coughed and stopped. I took the filter off, but could find no obstruction, though there must have been one, because on putting it back, Billy started up as if with gratitude. During his idleness we could see from fishing luggers (lying to anchors or their trawls) that we were being swept westwards. With Billy at work, we went about and once more approached the land. Sighted a harbour with big cranes, which Rouse hopefully declared must be Dover, but presently we saw the high bridge inland, and knew that it was Folkestone. The wind now shifted suddenly to the north, and freshened, and we were able to lay along the coast getting on well over the tide, with full sail, closehauled, and Billy at half throttle. Black clouds were gathering over the land and it grew oddly dark and began to rain. We reached Dover at about 8 pm, to find the tide still pouring out of the Western Entrance. I had meant to go in at the East Entrance, but after a good look at things, decided to go straight in here, turned on Billy full throttle and put her at it. We came in slowly, through a swirling tide, with uncanny patches of smooth in it. The steering was a little funny, but she was never in the least danger of being out of control. We then downed all sail in the outer harbour, motored into the Submarine Basin, and anchored in our old place, just south of the lifeboat. We were hardly in before the storm broke, with buckets of rain, thunder, and flashes of lightning so vivid that it was dazzling even to look at the cliffs and the harbour walls. The wind suddenly became very strong, N, working quickly round to SW. The flashes showed us swinging round and we spent a rocky night, rather anxious lest we should drag against the dock wall.

May 21. Bright sunshine, but strong SW wind, and white tops even in the good shelter of the Submarine Basin. Rouse got ashore with some difficulty in the afternoon and telephoned to his family. The wind moderated towards evening, and the barometer rose fast.

May 22. I woke at 5am and had a look round. The barometer had gone up another two tenths. Wind about SW, fresh. I woke Rouse and told him we'd start for home, put a plate of cornflakes and milk in front of him, and found him, as usual, ready for anything and eager to be off. We motored out of the Submarine Basin and hoisted sail (jib and single-reefed main), passed through the pierheads of the Eastern entrance at 6.15 am, shutting off Billy as soon as we were outside. At 6.50 the South Foreland bore WNW. We sailed very pleasantly through the Downs and passed the West Gull at 9.25. Weather forecast at 10.30 promised 'Fresh SW wind'. We had a good look at the North Foreland, sighted Longnose and rounded East Margate buoy. The wind was strengthening all the time, and between the N.E. Tongue and Pan Sand I rolled up the second reef, which eased her a good deal, and we made quick progress to the Girdler, which we reached at 1 pm. Visibility was now pretty bad and we had all the wind and sea we wanted. I was ridiculously bothered by finding the E. Red Sand buoy black and white, whereas, for some unknown reason, I had been expecting red and white. The colour was not marked on my chart. This was unpleasant in the mist, but we presently found the East Oaze buoy, which gave me once more the light conscience of a sure fix. All the way from the West Mouse to the Whitaker buoy we were on the verge of an accidental jibe, and did jibe purposely where necessary. I rolled down the third reef and steering became a great deal easier, while speed, if anything, increased.

Visibility began to improve, and from the Spitway lit buoy we could see not only the buoy at the other end of the swatch, but also one of the towers of Clacton in line with it. A nasty little sandy sea came after us through the swatch, and we rejoiced when at 4.35 we were through, and *Nancy*, with boom out to port, was foaming along for the Naze. We had Walton pier end-on at 6 pm, but after that had the flood tide against us till at 7.15 pm we passed the Beach End buoy (13 hours out from Dover). And so up the river to Pin Mill in time to come in for the tail end of a sausage and shanty party at the Butt and Oyster. It had been an extraordinarily pleasant and lucky little cruise. Harwich to Portsmouth and back between one Saturday and the next, with five nights in port and two at sea, and a whole day in Portsmouth and another in Dover. I daresay it will be a long time before winds and tides are so kind to us again.

PART TWO

After Ransome

CHAPTER SEVEN

After Ransome

യ

N*ancy Blackett* was sold in December 1938, to Reginald Russell, a fellow Pin Mill resident (no relation of George and Josephine), and an entertaining character in his own right. His daughter Gill used to crew for Ransome, and vividly recollects AR's wife, Evgenia: 'like a great walrus, sitting on the bunk in *Selina King* propped up against the table and smoking that awful pipe.' Russell's son Peter adds, 'With his eye for the fitness of things, my father was delighted that not only did she smoke a pipe, she smoked Capstan Full!' Ransome may have sold *Nancy*, but she did not easily let go of him. His log for 1 April 1939 records: 'Busy with *Nancy*. Sailed in her for an hour.'

Reggie Russell, *Nancy*'s new owner, described in her 'Blue Book' (Certificate of British Registry) as a merchant, was one of what were known as 'dirty shirt sailors' who had founded the Crouch Yacht Club in reaction against the more elitist Royal Burnham. He kept *Nancy* on a mooring off the end of the Hard at Pin Mill, and Peter recollects joining him to sail up and down the coast, from the Alde to the Crouch, during the summer of 1939, before the war intervened and *Nancy* was laid-up in a mud-berth just above Pin Mill for the duration. Reggie lost no time recommissioning *Nancy* at the end of the war, and spent VE night aboard her, fishing drunks out of the river. 'He sailed all that summer of 1945, living aboard and often alone all round those waters. The buoyage system had not yet been replaced, so he had to rely on fishermen's withies, and learn new marks on land where the channels had changed since 1939,' reports Peter. '*Nancy* went aground on mudbanks not infrequently.'

Peter recollects Ransome telling his father, 'You're in my next book,' though he never, at least identifiably, was. He also recalls AR 'cooking in *Nancy*'s little galley under the hatchway on the starboard side, where a sort of bicycle pump and a marrow-sized cylinder supplied paraffin vapour to either of two primus stoves,

his back to the little sink, breaking an egg into a can of tomato soup. When the egg looked right, the soup was ready too.'

Peter, who contacted the Nancy Blackett Appeal (forerunner of the Trust) soon after it was launched, also supplied two other items of interest. One was the address of Roger Fothergill, the man who as a teenager bought Swallow from Arthur Ransome in 1935 (see APPENDIX II). The other was Ransome's own carpet, from the cabin sole of *Nancy Blackett*, which he mentioned in a letter was rolled-up in his loft.

Two days later it arrived in the post, wrapped in a couple of taped-up bin bags. It proved to be a length of stair carpet, deep red, with a border and a geometric pattern, and a hole cut out, evidently to fit round the mast. Already it seemed naggingly familiar, and eventually I recalled the letter from Ransome to Taqui Altounyan, 'The Turkey carpet is all over fluff from bad rope-ends. You'd better come along and do some brushing.'

It was over a year before we had the chance to try laying the carpet in the newly-acquired *Nancy Blackett*. When we did, it fitted perfectly.

Following the war, Reggie moved *Nancy* to the Walton Backwaters, where the train service suited him better, and where she was looked after by Hall's of Walton-on-the-Naze. In 1952, ill-health prompted him to sell her.

Her new owner was Francis Knight. No relation, as far as I'm aware, to E. F. Knight, the author of Knight on *Sailing*, or of Frank Knight, the Woodbridge boatbuilder, he was a chartered accountant who lived in Clarges Street, off London's Piccadilly. He commissioned a survey from Norman Dallimore, well-known as a yacht designer of some quality. Many of his boats are still sailing, some built by King's at Pin Mill. His report begins by mentioning that, though he had never surveyed *Nancy* before, he had been aboard her some years previously, and had known Reggie Russell for some 45 years. He was a fellow-member of the Crouch Yacht Club.

The survey, handwritten in pencil, comments: 'I have heard that she was Hillyards' exhibition boat of 1931. She appears to have a little more finish than did most of Hillyards' boats of that date—she is planked with p[itch] pine.' It concludes: 'Finally, I am of opinion that this boat has been well looked-after for most of her life and was well put together when built. The materials were all of good quality and she only needs a good fit-out to put her in really good condition. She will outlast a lot of the post war boats.'

Frank and his wife Myfanwy were probably *Nancy*'s most adventurous owners, taking her to Denmark, via the Frisian Islands where *The Riddle of the Sands* was set, and frequently to Holland, often with a troupe of children aboard. They also made some modifications to her appearance, painting her hull black, which must have looked suitably piratical, and adding a boom-gallows—a horizontal wooden rest supported on a fixed frame—as an alternative to the scissor-like crutches. They continued to keep her in the Backwaters, with a mooring in the Twizzle, and a winter berth adjacent to the clubhouse of the Walton and Frinton Yacht Club—so close that in the great floods of 1953 her bowsprit poked the guttering off its eaves.

By 1957, pressure of work caused the Knights to regretfully sell *Nancy*, to a dashing and distinguished Naval Commander (later Captain) Bernard MacIntyre, who seems to have had more than a little of Commander Walker about him. Professionally, he had displayed enormous courage and leadership during the war, earning a DSC and Bar, as well as gaining a reputation for handling his ships with power and panache, and despising tugs. As a parent, his aim in buying *Nancy* was to provide his children with *Swallows and Amazons* style adventures. For his young son, Mark, these started with an act of apparent piracy before he realised they owned the boat. Rowing down the Twizzle, supposedly still looking for a boat to buy, Commander MacIntyire suddenly pointed to *Nancy*, said 'That one looks rather nice!' and to his son's horror, climbed aboard and started rummaging in her lockers.

MacIntyre restored *Nancy* to her *Goblin* look, white hull and tan sails. He also reinstated the *Goblin*-style paraffin primus stove—until it exploded and singed his eyebrows. He did however remove Ransome's 'little coke stove for people to bark their shins on', and in its place, at the head of Titty's bunk, installed a set of drawers which are still there.

The family got good use out of *Nancy*, still moored in the Backwaters. The parents read the Ransome stories to their children in the week, and re-enacted them on the boat at the weekends. They made one down-channel trip, getting as far as Newton Ferrers, in Devon. 'Westerlies going, and Easterlies coming back,' recalled Mark.

Nancy Blackett, as she was
found in Scarborough in the
1980s. Note the jet of water
from the leak in the hull, about
amidships (above).   Hatch,
porthole and engine gone, and
the cockpit destroyed (right).

All too soon, promotion and a posting to Germany forced MacIntyre to sell *Nancy*. In 1960 she was bought by George Batters, a 'conservator of forests'. Little more is known of him, apart from the facts that he removed *Nancy* to Scarborough, and that he had a Rolls-Royce, in which he delivered her gear to her next owner when he sold her five years later.

This new owner was William Bentley. He's listed in the Blue Book as a company director, and had been a house-builder. He later ran an antique shop in Scarborough—it's said he paid George Batters for *Nancy* with a mixture of cash and antique furniture. (He's been described as a greengrocer, but this appears to be solely on the basis of what happened to his shop after he left it.) He owned *Nancy* for 23 years and one week, between1965 and 1988, and has been reviled as the man who allowed her to deteriorate almost to the point of death. He did, but before that happened, he and his wife and children enjoyed many happy years with the boat.

Both of Bill Bentley's daughters have been in touch with the Trust in recent years, anxious to set the record straight. Sally Bell (now Furby) told me 'I was born in 1972 and spent the next decade sailing her every summer for my summer holidays. She was kept in first class condition at this time, I remember all our birthdays being put together and we forewent our presents to make sure we could pay the harbour dues for the year. My parents were not well off and lived on the breadline, everyone went without to make sure we could take her out every winter and store her and recaulk her… I remember at the age of seven helping shift all that smelly ballast one by one!'

Her elder sister Sarah visited *Nancy* at Woodbridge in the spring of 2013. As soon as she stepped aboard, she was transported back in time. '*Nancy* was my childhood,' she told me. 'Dad had a real passion for the boat—working on her and being at one with her was enough. Sailing her was a bonus, he always used to say—the cherry on the cake. He used to call it a bonus for all our hard work, her appreciation to us.'

Sarah, who was born just three years after *Nancy* came into the family, added, 'I grew up with *Nancy*. I was very close to my father during this time—he and I sailed and maintained her together. One of my jobs was polishing the oil lamps,'— which are still on board and in use—'not to mention lifting the ballast out of the bilges! There was never a day when I wasn't aboard her or thinking about her. I had many winters in the old goods yard sanding her hull and deck ready for a new coat of paint and varnish. I often used to sleep aboard her in the summer holidays. That was my bunk.' She pointed to the portside bunk in the forepeak, known to Ransome fans as Titty's bunk.

And yes, she recalls sailing to Holland with her dad. 'We went over when I was about eight, probably in 1976. Dad was an accomplished sailor, a talented and interesting individual who I admired for his many skills, most self-taught. He was very passionate when telling his stories of times sailing with my mother and friends.' He also cruised her as far as the Farne Islands to the north, and Aldeburgh to the south, but his favourite passage was a day-sail to Whitby and back. He also enjoyed racing *Nancy* locally, where she apparently acquitted herself well.

It's a picture of proud ownership and enthusiastic usage which was confirmed by Christina Hardyment when she went to visit *Nancy* for her 1984 book on Ransome's real-life influences, *Arthur Ransome and Captain Flint's Trunk*. She found a couple who delighted in *Nancy*'s Ransome associations, and were knowledgeable about her role in *We Didn't Mean to Go to Sea*. 'We've had some marvellous times in her,' the Bentleys told her. 'It's amazing how many people know her. Whenever we go into a new port, someone turns up who has seen her before, or who knew Ransome. She's an incredibly popular boat.'

Christina was also very taken with the boat herself. 'The cabin felt very roomy and high-ceilinged, and the whole little ship had a capable air, as if she was game for any adventure that might happen along. Very like Nancy herself, in fact.' She was intrigued by a story the Bentleys told of the occasional whiff of pipe tobacco in the cabin, as if Ransome's ghost still hung about the boat. *Nancy*, she summed-up, despite being painted green, 'was still her old self, and obviously in very capable hands.'

So what went wrong? Financial hardship and ill-health seem to have been the root cause. Sarah recalls that her last sail on *Nancy* was on Easter Saturday 1979, her 11th birthday. The Bentleys struggled to keep *Nancy* going—Sarah at one stage had a job in a hotel, chambermaiding and waitressing 'to put money in the *Nancy* pot'. But it was a losing battle. They could no longer afford to lift her out in the winters, and eventually started falling into arrears with the harbour dues.

Nancy soon began to deteriorate badly, the process augmented by a number of accidents. Both of her hatches were gone, one of them having been smashed when a car had been blown off the harbour wall in a gale, landing on top of her, and probably responsible for cracking several of her ribs as well.

In 1986, *Nancy* made the front page of Scarborough's *Evening News* when she broke loose from her moorings—it's thought children or teenagers had cast her off—and she drifted into a part of the harbour then called 'the pit', an area that was rarely dredged in those days. As the tide went out and *Nancy* settled on the bottom, her bilges found a metal spike sticking out of the harbour bed. It penetrated her hull, and she was sunk.

Although salvaged and tied-up again on the harbour wall, *Nancy* was battered, bruised and broken. Ribs and frames were smashed; her cockpit was an empty shell. Chafing, unfendered, against the harbour wall had worn away the planking on her port side. The weather blew through her uncovered hatchways and the tide filled and emptied through the hole in her hull.

By May 1988, *Nancy* was as good as a total wreck, lying on her side in the mud in the middle of the harbour. Scarborough Council, informed by the harbourmaster that she was a hazard to shipping, authorised her removal. It was thought she could be got up in one piece, and one of the councillors suggested she could be put to use, planted with flowers on the town's Marine Drive. They also considered contacting the Arthur Ransome Society to discuss her future, little knowing that at that time no such society existed—though oddly enough, *Nancy* would have a part to play in its formation not many years later.

Fortunately for *Nancy*, though, a saviour was at hand.

CHAPTER EIGHT

Restoration

❧

To this day, Mike Rines swears he doesn't know what make him want to rescue and restore *Nancy Blackett*. He was a sailor, but he already had a perfectly serviceable boat—a modern glassfibre catamaran, which provided stable, comfortable upright cruising in the worst of weathers—quite the opposite of a single-hulled cutter like *Nancy Blackett*—and which required very little maintenance compared with a sixty-year-old wooden boat. Furthermore, he had never read an Arthur Ransome book in his life, and had no inkling of the significance of the Nancy Blackett name.

But Mike had an eye for a pretty boat, and twenty years earlier he had first seen and, he says, coveted the smart little green-painted cutter. He lived nearly 200 miles away from Scarborough, but regularly visited his parents there, and had noted with distress *Nancy*'s decline. Eventually he decided to step in and try to save her, but his initial overtures to her owner met with rebuff. Bill Bentley's daughter Sarah recalls that it was in 1985 that her father first mentioned Mike Rines phoning him. Apparently many people had contacted Bill Bentley seeking to buy *Nancy*, but he was still stubbornly attached to her and turned them all away. 'My father was in denial, and hoped that somehow we could turn things round,' was daughter Sally's reading of the situation. But his resolve was slowly worn down as *Nancy* continued to decline. 'The car incident just about killed him off,' said Sally, a few years before his death at the age of 82 in 2010. 'She was his pride and joy and it pains him to talk about her even now.'

Mike's patience and persistence—perhaps assisted by an ultimatum from the Council and Bill Bentley's own failing health—eventually won the day. 'Dad I'm sure always felt he let us down in some way by letting *Nancy* go, but I'd say 'No dad you've saved her, she will be there for many more to enjoy her and that is a good thing',' said his daughter Sarah.

Mike paid £1,000 to have *Nancy* lifted out—salvaged is probably the more appropriate term—and inspected. The estimate for her repairs was over £7,000, so he agreed to pay Bill Bentley £3,000, plus any change from the £7,000 if the repairs came in under that sum. In the event, they came a great deal more, but that is getting a little ahead of the story.

On 25 August 1988, Mike and his wife Ann were registered as the joint owners of *Nancy Blackett*, and, as Mike put it later on, 'On a bright September morning, *Nancy* returned home.' Much closer to home, in a way, than anyone, least of all Mike himself at one time, realised. Mike lived at the time near the River Orwell, in Suffolk, in the grounds of Broke Hall, the same Broke Hall that had been home to Ransome's young friends George and Josephine Russell, and little more than half a mile from Broke Farm, the Ransomes' own home when Arthur owned *Nancy*. He could see the farmhouse (nowadays called Broke House) from his study window. Even more intriguingly, Mike's house was a conversion of two outbuildings joined by an infill section which had been built right on the old footpath connecting the farm to the hall. Ransome must have often walked right through Mike's own home.

In another seemingly-propitious coincidence, when Mike, then a magazine editor, had first discovered *Nancy*, he had casually mentioned the boat to his deputy editor, a keen sailor, although without using her name, which seemed to him at the time of no significance. She said it sounded very like the one she had grown up with, called *Nancy Blackett*—she was Clico MacIntyre, daughter of Commander MacIntyre, *Nancy*'s previous owner but three.

Nancy arrived on a low-loader and was delivered to Fox's marina on the Orwell, a few miles upriver from Pin Mill—they were pleased to see her and provided space in the yard rent-free. She arrived, as boats do, with some accessories. They included old flares, which were disposed of, a 10-man liferaft from an Icelandic trawler, a 10ft sweep and a linen map of the Walton Backwaters, believed to be post-war, and now framed and hanging in the Ship Inn at Levington. A used contraceptive was also found aboard, an indignity probably visited on the poor boat when she lay open to all with her hatches gone.

Mike engaged a shipwright, seventy-year-old Dunkirk veteran Stan Ball, to tackle the carpentry. As well as four cracked frames and twenty-six ribs, he re-

Mike Rines and shipwright Stan Ball consult *We Didn't Mean to Go to Sea* for guidance

placed an eighth of the pitch-pine planking, part of the transom and some of the deck planking. The cockpit, which had virtually gone, along with the engine, leaving the frames exposed by the time Mike took *Nancy* over, had to be rebuilt. Both the main hatch and fore hatch were missing and had to be replaced.

As is often the case with restorations, more work than Mike had bargained for materialised. The keel proved to have corroded in a number of places; the rudder had to be replaced, and the mast and bowsprit turned out to be cracked. A new engine and propulsion system were needed—the reconditioned engine that Mike found still carried the Thornycroft name, but was a diesel, made in Japan by Mitsubishi and considerably larger and more powerful then Ransome's little 'Handy Billy'. The list of items needing replacement continued to grow: propeller, water and fuel tanks, bilge pump, most metal fittings and blocks, the standing and running rigging, anchor and chain. The interior, much modified by Bill Bentley, was stripped-out, and Mike, by now thoroughly immersed in Arthur Ransome, referred to the drawings in *We Didn't Mean to Go to Sea* to get the cabin layout, as well as details of the deck fittings and rigging, right. New blue-covered bunk cushions went in, as well as a Taylor's paraffin stove, as Ransome had had, but with a pressurised tank for the paraffin in the lazarette, rather than on a cabin bulkhead. A replacement for the round washing-up basin was fashioned by fitting a plug-hole in an enamel bowl. The old brass paraffin lamps, though, went back in—and are still there.

Towards the end of the refit, Stan Ball left the project, and the UK, to travel to New Zealand to join his daughter. His replacement was found by a fortunate chance, when a boat that had come adrift from its moorings was blown ashore in a gale near Mike's home. Mike's son tied the errant vessel to a tree, enquiries were made locally, and a day or so later, the owner arrived at Mike's front door with a bottle of wine to say thanks. He proved to be a young, newly-qualified naval architect called James Pratt who lived locally and had just finished restoring the boat. When Mike asked him if he'd like to work on *Nancy Blackett*, he jumped at the chance.

By June 1989, *Nancy*'s hull had been repainted, back to the original gleaming white, and her superstructure varnished. The rudder remained to be hung, and there was much fitting-out still to be done inside but she was, externally at least, sufficiently her old self to be exhibited, ashore, at the East Coast Boat Show, held in her home boatyard, Fox's, where she proved a star attraction.

To mark this milestone in *Nancy*'s restoration, Mike decided to organise a celebration dinner—and where better to hold it than at the Butt and Oyster in Pin Mill, Ransome's 'local' when he lived on the Orwell, and the self-same pub, introduced quite casually in *We Didn't Mean to Go to Sea* when Jim remarks, at seven o'clock in the evening, 'I'll see what the Butt can do me by way of breakfast.'

Quite possibly the dinner was, apart from the actual rescue and restoration of *Nancy*, Mike's greatest contribution to the Ransome revival. He brought together a veritable A-list assemblage of Ransome people—those who had known him, or written about him, or had simply been passionate in their enthusiasm for him. They were people whom Mike had encountered or contacted in the course of his researches around *Nancy* during the course of her restoration.

Heading the table were three of the Altounyan siblings, on whom the Walker children, the Swallows, were, more or less, based. Inconveniently for Ransome, the offspring of his old friends Ernest and Dora Altounyan, whom he had taught to sail in the real *Swallow*, and for whom he wrote the first book 'in return for a pair of slippers', consisted of three girls, and a boy, and what the demands of fiction required were two of each. So Taqui, the eldest, became a boy, John, in the books, but everyone agrees that there's a lot of her high-spirited character in Nancy Blackett, Terror of the Seas and 'master and part-owner of the Amazon'. As a schoolgirl Taqui sailed with Ransome in *Nancy*, and he enrolled her as a cadet member of the Cruising Association, where, at the age of 19—so the story goes—she went to its annual ball, in a black taffeta dress, with a rose in her hair, and danced all night with Uffa Fox. Susie lent her name, though not much else of her personality, to the sensible mother-surrogate Susan Walker in the books. Absent were Titty, the third-eldest and 'able-seaman' of the books, who did not come, and Roger, ship's boy, who had developed the asthma treatment Intal, and the 'Spinhaler' to deliver it, and who had died, prematurely and possibly as a result of self-inflicted medical experiments, in 1987. Brigit, the youngest by quite a gap, was also at the dinner. She was represented as the baby 'fat Vicky' in *Swallows and Amazons*, but appears under more or less her own name as the 'ship's baby' Bridget in *We*

Nancy's interior, what's left of it, looking forward (note the missing planks)

Didn't Mean to Go to Sea and especially in *Secret Water* where she at last has a starring role.

Also present were a number of people who had written about Ransome: Christina Hardyment, whose *Arthur Ransome and Captain Flint's Trunk*, and Hugh Brogan, whose definitive Life of Arthur Ransome had both been published (by AR's own publisher, Cape) in 1984, to mark the centenary of his birth. Roger Wardale, a Bognor schoolteacher, had already written several books about Ransome, and would go on to write more, including the sailing memoir which borrowed the name of the *Nancy Blackett* for its title (it was published in 1991 with the subtitle 'Under Sail with Arthur Ransome'; after being out of print for a number of years, a revised and updated version, simply called *Arthur Ransome Under Sail*, was launched by another publisher in 2010).

Brian Hammett, a leading figure in the Cruising Association, of which Ransome had been a member (and its honorary port officer for Riga), would subsequently edit for publication the long-lost *Racundra's Third Cruise*, and re-edit with additional material, the original edition of *Racundra's First Cruise*.

And there were a good many people who had known Ransome personally. John Berry had been a friend of the Ransomes and the Altounyans since he knocked at the door of the latter's home, Lanehead, in 1958 during a search for the 'originals' of the books. Josephine Russell, the schoolgirl Ransome had met with her brother George when they were living at Broke Hall in the 1930s, and who had regularly crewed *Nancy*, was there. As was John Bell, an old friend of Ransome (he had married Pamela Whitlock, co-author of *The Far Distant Oxus*, which Ransome had championed with his publisher) and subsequently his literary executor.

Several members of the Rouse family came, relatives of Philip Rouse, the congenial sailing companion with whom Ransome undertook the 'Saturday to Saturday' voyage to Portsmouth and back.

One of the guests with the shortest distance to come was Martin Lewis, a local sailor and member of the Pin Mill Sailing Club who, as a boy, had cycled from his home in Ipswich to call on Ransome at Levington. Martin was never one to stint himself where his enthusasms were concerned. A fan of the theatre and the ballet, his house up the hill in Chelmondiston was full of old programmes, signed photos and mementoes. As a young Ransome fan he would bombard the author with letters asking—or, one suspects, putting him right—about aspects of sailing. It was at his funeral that I heard one of the best Martin stories. His mother answered their door in Ipswich one day to find a portly gentleman on the step, who announced: 'My name's Ransome. I've brought a copy of my latest book for Martin—and would you please ask him to stop writing to me.'

Living even closer to the Butt were Ron and Hetty Watts, who inhabit part of the building that had been Alma Cottage, though not the forward-jutting wing that still bears the name. The Altounyan 'girls' were staying with them.

One of Ransome's later boats, *Peter Duck*, was represented by her owner Greg Palmer, who as a teenager had been one of the many youngsters to have taught themselves to sail by reading *Swallows and Amazons*, and who with his wife Ann had bought the boat less than two years previously.

Jim Lawrence, legendary East Coast barge skipper and sailmaker, was there and so was the Rev Bill Broad who had founded the Cirdan Sailing Trust, which operates a small fleet of traditional sailing boats for young people on the East Coast—it was thought *Nancy* might join them, but she proved too small for that to be practicable.

In all, some thirty people were there. Many, though diehard Ransome fans, had never actually met each other before, so perhaps it was not surprising that the conversation turned to the idea of forming an Arthur Ransome Society. Within a few months the catalyst for such an organisation came in the form of a public appeal, launched by Christina Hardyment, to save another significant Ransome boat. This was *Amazon*, or as she was called in real life, *Mavis*, the dinghy owned by the Altounyans, which had sparred with *Swallow*, and AR himself, on Coniston, and provided the other half of the inspiration for *Swallows and Amazons*. She had been lovingly but erroneously encased in glassfibre by Ernest Altounyan himself in an effort to preserve her, but now she was rotting away inside this sheath. The response to the appeal was swift and generous, and it was the contributors who formed the basis of the Society, which held its inaugural meeting at the Windermere Steamboat Museum at the end of June, 1990. The event included a renaming ceremony for the partly-restored *Amazon* (ex-*Mavis*); appropriately the honour of smashing the bottle of grog against her prow went to Katy Jennings, a

Scarborough schoolgirl who, when she had heard about *Nancy*'s restoration, had written to Mike Rines, begging to help sail her to Holland, and who a year previously had persuaded her father to drive her all the way to Ipswich, to see *Nancy Blackett* in her partly-restored state at the boat show.

By then, mid-1990, *Nancy*'s own restoration was complete. She was back at the East Coast Boat Show, but this time, afloat. Just. Two summers, and two mild, dry winters had opened her seams and when she entered the water, the water began to enter her. Fortunately her planks quickly took up, and by the time the show opened, the inrush had reduced to a weep.

Outwardly, she was Arthur Ransome's 'best little boat' again: gleaming white hull, tan sails, mast-hoops, and the boom resting once more in scissor-like crutches. Below, too, the cabin was restored to its former glory, with its original brass paraffin lamps, its paraffin stove, its sink and the blue mattresses on the bunks.

But *Nancy*, now that she had been brought back to life, and felt the water beneath her keel, was becoming restless again. The first issue of the newly-formed Arthur Ransome Society's journal, *Mixed Moss*, which came out that autumn, carried a full-page advertisement on its inside back cover. 'NANCY BLACKETT (alias *Goblin*) restored faithfully to her 1930s condition, sails again on the Orwell. Now, his task completed, owner Michael Rines reluctantly has to sell her—preferably to another Ransome fan.'

The truth was that *Nancy*'s restoration had gone vastly over budget. The £7,000 estimate had stretched, over the two years of work, to nearly £40,000. Mike had painstakingly and carefully restored her to her original appearance—he had even sourced a brass pump for the cockpit—but now he had no option but to try and square the financial circle by putting *Nancy* on the market. Once again, it was time for her to move on.

The Great Race

TARS Rally, Woolverstone–junta–Pin Mill, Saturday 14 May 1994
by Martin Lewis

Tributes first. A barbecued billygoat for Colin Winter, owner of *Nancy Blackett* (alias *Goblin*), who gave East Anglian TARS free use of her although he himself was away in the Channel Islands. A suffering lamprey to Peter Roche whose indefatigable energy organised the whole rally in meticulous detail and who sailed *Nancy Blackett* solo under main alone from Pin Mill to the Marina at Woolverstone in the frisky Friday easterly breeze (while I pursued him in imp-sized *Nipper* under oars.) And a jib boom and bobstay memento for Richard Woodman, Marine Superintendent for Trinity House at Harwich, for supervising the whole race from the handsome *Andromeda* with his wife Christine and a crowded crew of eight other able seamen. Taking part in the race, besides the *Nancy Blackett* with Peter, myself (navigator) and four more worthies, were the Vertue *Patience* skippered by Ian Wright and a crew of three sea salts, Greg and Anne Palmer's *Peter Duck* (plus seven), the Mirouge *Dawn Treader,* Mike and Mary Shepherd with the Tyes and the Paulls, and John and Tricia Cesarini in their smart *Gaudio*.

I was delighted to see in what good shape the *Nancy Blackett* looked. I knew how meticulously Mike Rines had restored her and now learnt she had just had a thorough refit over the winter at Southwold before her return to Pin Mill, where, I might add, she has a mooring in a prime position just off the end of the Hard. *Nancy* is an old lady, a pensioner of 63 years, so you cannot expect a boat show finish of a modern fibreglass production model complete with all the latest navigational devices and every imaginable luxury for leisure living. She does in fact have terylene sails and epoxy composition decking. Electric navigation lights nestle alongside her paraffin ones which cannot shine the requisite mileage, and an echo sounder and VHF are discreetly hidden behind a varnished wood panel.

But otherwise she remains a sturdy, gracious pre-war working yacht, gleaming varnishwork on solid wood. She's all wood and what a business it must be to keep every plank, timber and fitting cleanly in paint and varnish. And so it is. There are oil lamps, all in gimbals, for light in the cabins and these could have done with an eager crew of Swallows to burnish them up brightly. And I was fascinated to see the little brass condensation cups under each porthole to catch the water from the glass from dripping onto the bunks below. I was indeed thrilled to see her fitted out and finished with such loving care, the devotion of a true seaman who respects his craft, knows her worth and invests in her, not fancy frills but plain solid workmanship, a sheer joy to behold and touch.

At half past twelve (one bell in the Afternoon Watch) the crews were briefed, complete with photocopied charts; the course was to be from a Pin Mill start down river against wind and tide to Shotley Spit, turn up the Stour to the turning mark, Bristol Buoy off the Bristol Arms, Shotley and back to Pin Mill via Shotley Spit again. I take the Great Race from *Nancy/Goblin*'s and my viewpoint from now on.

The morning had been the same frisky four-to-five easterly as the previous day and we had cautiously put three rolls in the main (using the little brass handle just as John had) and confined our headsails to stays'l only. But even as we headed down to Pin Mill the weather was changing. It was clouding over and drizzle and rain came up and the wind fell to a steady force three but still in the east. We struggled into oilskins, let out the reefs and set the jib out on the bowsprit end.

Sailing *Nancy/Goblin* we soon found out she is not the tiny boat Arthur implied. Seven tons Thames Measurement is no tiddler; she's twenty-eight feet long plus a ferocious bowsprit. She was and is eminently a North Sea-going yacht not just an estuary creek-hopping ditch crawler. Holy Catfish, we looked across at *Patience*, a Vertue, three feet shorter and much the same build; why, David Lewis had sailed his Vertue, *Cardinal Vertue*, across the Atlantic in the first Single Handed Trans Atlantic Race in 1960.

Another point we noticed was the comparative small size of the two headsails, stays'l and jib, compared with the vast genoas modern boats fly and, consequent on this, the absence of any winches with which to bowse in the sheets. It was just a straight pull to the cleats.

: The author, sailing *Nancy Blackett* home from her first Ipswich Festival in 1997

2: Being restored by Mike Rines in Fox's marina, 1988

3: Original Swallows, Altounyan sisters Brigit, Taqui and Susa

NANCY BLACKETT

At the restoration dinner: Hugh Brogan, Roger Wardale, Christina Hardyment

5: Winter working party at Harbour Marine, 1998

6: Our first, impromptu, show stand, Maritime Ipswich, 1997

7: "What's the furthest you've ever been in her?" *Nancy* in Falmouth, 199

8: "A boat close to my heart": NBT patron Ellen MacArthur in *Nancy*'s cabin

9: In Flushing (Vlissingen) harbour

10: Expecting visitors at a St Katharine Docks festiv

11: With the cast of Eastern Angles' *We Didn't Mean to Go to Sea*, 2016

12: School group with skipper Bryan Bonser

13: *Nancy* on the Orwell with her new mast, 2017

It was long and short down to Collimer where the river bends south and *Dawn Treader* and *Gaudio* soon vanished into the misty murk ahead never to be seen again. With my 'local knowledge' we poked out of tide over the dreaded Potter Point shallows but with our safety net of the echo sounder set to bleep at eight feet (we drew about four). Having sailed bilge-keelers most of my sailing life, I suddenly became aware that I had a real deep-keeled yacht under me, gripping the water and making ground resolutely over both wind and tide. A puff and she heeled sharply but safely over. I heard a crash below as a shower of books fell off the shelf and loose gear left on the bunks cascaded into a confusion on the cabin floor.

There was rain and drizzle but I can't say I noticed it much. I could feel the tremor of the ship through the tiller; with full sail she was nicely balanced and I felt her respond to my touch of the helm. Perched on the quarter seat, I peered over the cabin top and concentrated on close hauled sailing. The others in the cockpit sort of faded from my consciousness and for a spell I was, like John, alone with my craft, biting into the waves, making up to windward with each puff, bearing away to keep her moving in the lulls. *Up and back. Up and back. Good little ship.* I put a hand over the edge of the coaming and patted the damp deck. Despite the rainy damp I was unashamedly happy and a grin of sheer delight spread across my face. I was actually sailing, not the *Nancy Blackett*, but *Goblin*, real live, pulsating, windward-making *Goblin*. In my and her home waters, the River Orwell.

As we approached Collimer my trick at the helm was up. We had pulled steadily away from *Peter Duck* and *Patience* on the close haul and kept our lead round Collimer as we freed our sheets for a swirling reach with the wind abeam. I knew my river in the mist and we were able to cut over the Fagbury shallows while the others more cautiously kept to deeper water but in the foul tide too. We surged round Shotley Spit, let off the backstays and let out the sheets for our run up the Stour, goose winged with the stays'l held out to windward on the boathook. But now the gaffers behind us, their gaff mains swung squarely out to take full advantage of the following wind, began to make up on us. By Bristol Buoy *Peter Duck* had squeezed ahead of us and *Patience* was on our tail.

Back from Bristol to Shotley Spit we were tacking against wind and the last of the flood and once again dropped *Patience* behind and nearly made up to

Peter Duck. We both had to put in a short extra tack to make the mark which we rounded almost together but, once round, *Peter Duck* picked up her skirts and fairly flew away from us. And the Vertue came steadily, patiently indeed, up from astern. Tide turned and the wind fell away. Progress through Buttermans Bay became slower and slower and *Patience* sat on our lee quarter, surging up alongside every now and again but falling back again as we took his wind. Approaching the red stud of Fox's Bottom the crafty Ian found a light weather jib and hoisted it upside down up to the hounds, creeping through to loo'ard at last and taking line honours from us. *Andromeda* called three cheers for *Patience* and, a few moments later, three cheers for the *Nancy Blackett*. But for me it was ten million cheers for *Goblin*.

CHAPTER NINE

An Excellent Plan

❦

Fast forward now to 1996. It's the Easter weekend, and we're redecorating our younger daughter's bedroom. *Signals*, the newsletter of the Arthur Ransome Society, has arrived, and I pick it up during a coffee break. A small announcement at the bottom of one of the East Anglian regional pages catches my eye.

Headed 'Ransome's 'best little boat' up for sale', it reads simply: '*Nancy Blackett* is up for sale, again. Anyone interested, contact [telephone number]. Price £30,000.' I pick up the phone…

In fact I made two calls, one to Peter Roche, chairman of TARS East Anglian region, to get some background, the other to the number given in the notice, which proved to be that of the then owner of *Nancy*, Colin Winter, who had bought her from Mike Rines in 1991. Thus was set in chain a process—part task, part challenge, part adventure, part administrative nightmare—which was to have a profound effect on my own life, but more importantly, on that of the *Nancy Blackett*.

Quite why I was moved to take this single, momentous step along what has proved to be an immensely long path I still don't really know. I suppose I argued with myself that it would be a shame if nobody made the move to secure her future, so perhaps I'd better, and then if anybody else was interested, nothing would have been lost. As to why I thought it would be a shame, all I can say is that, like Mike Rines, I've always had an eye for a pretty boat. And I've also been especially fascinated by those special places and objects that link the world of fiction with that of real life.

At this time, I had only seen *Nancy Blackett* the once, about two yerars previously, in 1994, when I'd travelled to the River Orwell for an event billed as the 'Great Race' between *Nancy* and *Peter Duck*. This event had been organized by Peter Roche for TARS East. Colin Winter had kindly loaned him *Nancy* for the

The 'Great Race' of 1994: *Peter Duck*, right, is leading *Nancy Blackett*

day and the race was officiated by local yachtsman and author Richard Woodman. It resulted in a win for *Peter Duck*. It had also left me deeply moved by the sight of *Nancy*, and the literary significance of her presence here, where the opening scenes of one of my favourite books are set. I had already become familiar with *Nancy*'s romantic history through Roger Wardale's book *Nancy Blackett: Under Sail with Arthur Ransome*.

Surely, I now reasoned, there would be a sufficient groundswell of enthusiasm among Arthur Ransome fans to raise the money to buy her. Colin, who lived, promisingly enough, in a house called Holly Howe, was willing to hold *Nancy* while I made some further inquiries and arrangements.

Already I was formulating a plan whereby the Arthur Ransome Society (TARS for short), would buy *Nancy*, look after her, enable members to sail on her, and take her to festivals and exhibitions, as a literal flagship for TARS, Ransome and his books. Of course, we would recreate the voyage of the *Goblin* across the North Sea to Flushing—perhaps not crewed exclusively by children, but these were details that could be worked out. There would inevitably be lots of details, but the basic plan was beautifully simple, and obviously desirable—or as Ransome himself might have put it, 'gorgeous, inevitable and handed out on a plate'.

All that needed to happen was for the idea to be suggested—once that happened, everyone would be enthused by it and the powers that be within TARS, the management committee, mandated by the membership, would take the necessary action. I knew that TARS had funds in reserve, about £17,000 I thought, not enough in itself, but a good start and coupled with an appeal, and a bit of fundraising (and why not the Heritage Lottery Fund?) we could get there. I had also heard that the reserves were being built up with a view to one day being able to buy a Ransome property or artefact. And what better piece of Ransome heritage than something distinctive, large and recognisable which spanned both his life and his literature—his favourite boat and star of one of his finest books?

I immediately drafted a letter outlining the plan and asking for comments, and sent it off to about eighty of the more active and influential members who I thought might, or ought to be, interested in the idea. The response was immediate. Numerous people wrote back, mostly expressing enthusiasm, some enclosing cheques. My own TARS Southern Region, of which I'd been a committee member for some time, offered to sponsor the project, and its treasurer, Diana Sparkes, promptly opened a bank account in the name of the Nancy Blackett Appeal.

My immediate target became the forthcoming TARS International AGM, to be held over the Spring Bank Holiday weekend at the end of May. TARS had adopted a regional structure, with six regions (Scottish, Northern, Midlands, Eastern, Southern—mine—and South West) which rotated the organisation of the social weekend around the IAGM between them. This year it was the turn of the South West, and the event was being held in Bristol to coincide with the first International Festival of the Sea which was taking place there. One of the first to respond to my letters was Albert Hicken, South West chairman and a keen yachtsman himself, who was busy organising the 1996 AGM weekend to be held in Bristol over the late May Bank Holiday.

Albert and I spent many hours on the phone trying to work out how we could get *Nancy* from Southwold, where she was based at the time, to the festival. It was too late to sail her round, even if she was up to it and we had the crews. Transport by road was not an option—too bone-shaking, and too expensive. At one stage we got as far as comparing her draught with the depth of the Kennett and Avon Canal—it might just have worked but parts of the canal, which was in the process of restoration, were still impassable so that was that. In the end we settled for printing up some flyers and making a large placard, to be displayed on the TARS stand at the festival, and at the formal AGM on the Sunday afternoon.

Nancy's possible acquisition—'saving' or 'rescuing' her as some people put it—was the talk of the AGM campsite, and the Saturday-night social, a rousingly and fittingly nautical affair featuring the splendid Bristol Shantymen. And it caught the attention of visitors to the Festival, with expressions of enthusiasm, and even some donations—including one particularly touching contribution from an unknown schoolboy who emptied his pockets to contribute £1.62 for *Nancy*.

But the AGM itself proved a harder nut to crack. The agenda had been laid down weeks before and there was no changing it now. Eventually, however, space was allowed under Any Other Business, and I put the proposal, in effect that TARS should buy and maintain the *Nancy Blackett*. To my surprise and consternation there turned out to be a good deal of opposition to this self-evidently right and sensible idea. The argument was essentially between those who thought that we should take the opportunity (or 'Grab a chance' as we didn't hesitate to put it) to safeguard *Nancy*'s future, and those who felt that it couldn't be done, not by TARS at any rate. The debate raged. We raised the prospect of *Nancy*, in private hands, deteriorating again as she had done in Scarborough. They suggested that it would be best to hope that she would be purchased by a (purely hypothetical) private individual who would be sympathetic to TARS having a look at her once in a while. We countered with the possibility of this individual being a reclusive collector in whose hands she might disappear, possibly abroad. This was not entirely hypothetical—it had been suggested to us (whether with any truth, I never found out) that Hergé, the Belgian creator of TinTin, was interested.

The argument grew warm. I well remember Aidan de la Mare, a tall, bearded sailor with a penchant for cruising in open dinghies, standing with arm outstretched and finger pointing like an old man of the sea to denounce Jim Andrews for being faint-hearted (and possibly lily-livered). Jim, an Ulsterman with a terrier-like streak, and no mean sailor, and yachting author, himself, was firmly convinced the project was impossible—though a few years later, he came round 180 degrees and became one of the Trust's most fervent supporters.

It became clear early on in the debate that the National Committee was not going to declare itself in favour of the project. However, the level of support in the hall meant that the idea was not going to fade away, and an impasse began to develop. Its resolution came in the form of an amendment proposed by Roger Wardale, that TARS wished 'fair winds and a prosperous voyage' to those wishing to purchase the *Nancy Blackett*.

Initially I found this disappointing, and not without irony—Roger, then chairman of the Southern Region, was the first TARS Member I had met when I and my family joined the society in 1993. We'd seen in the regional newsletter that there was to be a walk up Beacon Hill near Newbury and, rather uncharacteristically for a family of non-joiners-in had decided to go along, and introduce ourselves to the group. This tall, craggy man, in an Arthur Ransome Club of Japan sweatshirt, seemed indefinably to be in charge so we marched up to him and said hello. That was Roger. It was a memorable day—there were about thirty or so people who proved to be an amiable, chatty bunch, many of whom subsequently became firm friends. At one stage as we rambled up the hill, I found myself chatting to the ur-John/Nancy herself, Taqui Altounyan. At of the end of the walk, from the little bookstall in the boot of an estate car, I bought a book. Unusually for me, then, it was a hardback, but the bookstall man, Ted Alexander, assured me it would be much more durable than a paperback, which turned out to have been just as well. It was Roger's book, *Nancy Blackett: Under Sail with Arthur Ransome*, which I immediately got signed by the author.

And now, here he was, the very man who had inspired and informed my passion for this boat, proposing this wet, off-the-hook sort of compromise motion. In retrospect, though, it proved to be the wisest pointer for the future. While it closed the door on any of TARS' supposed wealth, it left those of us who wanted to buy *Nancy* free to develop the project as we saw fit—and, though we did not know it then, TARS was about to enter a troubled period which would have left it with neither the time nor the financial freedom to attend to a project as large and demanding as the *Nancy Blackett*.

The motion was carried, the meeting moved on and eventually ended. As we left the hall, my spirits were lifted by the number of people who came up to me to promise support and, in many cases to press cash and cheques into my hand. But my ordeal was not entirely over. Straight after the AGM was a National Committee meeting, to which I had previously been invited to set out my proposals for *Nancy*. And a gruesome, bad-tempered event it turned out to be—not particularly on my account, I think. It just, for some reason, was. But when it came to my turn to make my pitch, most sympathisers seemed to have decided to keep their heads well down. The President, Brigit Sanders (née Altounyan) struck a supportive note, but the result, following the AGM, seemed a foregone conclusion. Whatever happened to the *Nancy Blackett*, it would not be happening under the banner of TARS. One member went so far as to suggest that any *Nancy Blackett* publicity material should be required to carry a statement that it was not connected to TARS, but this was shouted down, and perhaps as a reaction to this, as it seemed, gratuitously malevolent piece of hostility, the committee voted a sum of £100 towards setting-up costs.

As we left Bristol, in our rented camper-van, I reflected that at least we now knew where we stood. We could expect some support, but not much, from TARS as an organisation—predictble, really, as it was in line with the approach to other,

A young fan visits *Nancy* at Brundall Bay on the Broads in the summer of 1996

considerably less costly projects such as the restoration of another Ransome boat, the dinghy *Coch-y-bonddhu*. At least the goodwill was worth something, and we now had a better idea who our friends, and our enemies, were. So we were free to set up our own operation. We'd raised a bit more money, and, best of all, the mass support and enthusiasm I'd hoped for, and without which the thing would undoubtedly not work, was undoubtedly there.

The next move was obviously to set up a steering committee of our own, and begin figuring out what sort of organisational structure, and what kind of fund-raising campaign we needed, but there were a few incidents during the summer which boosted morale—we heard from Josephine Russell, who as a teenager had sailed with Ransome in *Nancy*, and also from Peter Russell, no relation to Josephine, but son of Reggie Russsell, to whom Ransome had sold *Nancy*. He sent Ransome's original carpet from *Nancy*'s cabin sole, the one about which he'd written to Taqui Altounyan, 'the Turkey carpet is all over fluff from bad rope ends. You'd better come along and do some brushing'.

Peter also introduced us to Roger Fothergill, who as a young man, had bought the original *Swallow* from Ransome (and unfortunately sold her on again soon after, whereupon she'd become lost to posterity). Mike Rines produced copious photographs, as well as various bits and pieces of *Nancy* left over from the restoration, among them around 200 boatbuilders' copper nails which he had pulled out of the planking in the course of the work. Film-maker Charles Mapleston, who had made a charming half-hour documentary on *Nancy*'s restoration for Anglia TV, arranged the permissions to enable us to run off a limited edition of videos for fund-raising.

And in early August, I had a phone-call from Colin Winter, *Nancy*'s owner, to ask if we would like to man her for a day at the Vintage Wooden Boat Association's rally later in the month. He had a conflicting appointment and we could open her up and show visitors around if we liked. I phoned my friend Andy Morley and with three of his children, we made our way the following Saturday afternoon to—rather improbably—Brundall Bay Marina on the Norfolk Broads.

The following morning provided a foretaste of many events to come. We tidied the boat, set the kids to polishing the brasswork, opened the doors and waited. Soon we were inundated with visitors, most of them Ransome fans, and all highly appreciative. One particular little girl, aged eleven or twelve, darted aboard and, obviously thrilled to bits to be aboard the *Goblin*, ticked-off all the items on the boat that she remembered from the book, including the brass reefing-handle, the compass porthole, the washing-up bowl the blue mattresses, and—the ultimate test of the true fan—which bunk was whose. We were equally delighted. It confirmed our belief that *Nancy* would mean something to all generations.

The next time I saw *Nancy* was in the autumn; she was out of the water, propped up on legs outside the shed at Harbour Marine in Southwold. It was pouring with rain, and four of us, Martin Lewis, Doug Faunt from the US, Paul Crisp (TARS Southern chairman) and myself, clambered up the ladder and crowded into her cabin to hold the first formal meeting of the Nancy Blackett Appeal steering committee. We decided that we should become a registered charity (which we would do before launching a major appeal for funds, in order to enjoy the tax relief on personal donations), planned to look into applying to the Heritage Lottery Fund, and to acquaint ourselves with the regulations that would apply to any sailing activities we might envisage.

By the following spring, most of the groundwork for setting up the charitable trust was in place, thanks to advice in particular from the Norfolk Heritage Fleet (Hunters Yard) which had recently carried out a similar exercise on a much larger scale, and with the help of the legal advice team at the National Council for Voluntary Organisations, who advised that we should become a 'company limited by guarantee' and helped draw up the necessary Memorandum and Articles.

It was at that point, 24 April to be precise, that I had another phone-call from Colin Winter. It seemed his personal finances had taken a turn for the worse, and he needed to sell *Nancy* quickly—indeed if she were not sold, she might end up being seized by a creditor, and there was one who would be only too glad to do so. He could give us four weeks. Five at the most. But he would drop the price to £25,000.

At that stage we had about £2,000 in the kitty, donated by the 200 or so people who were on the mailing list of what we were calling the Friends of *Nancy Blackett*. Several had indicated they would be willing to donate more, when the time was ripe. Now, regardless of our yet-to-be achieved charitable status, it seemed it was. We immediately rushed out a letter to these supporters, and asked

TARS for the use of its mailing list of about 1,800 names. It responded swiftly and positively. Even so, it took about a week to set things up, and by the time we drafted this new, wider, letter, which included a personal message from Brigit, TARS president and by now patron of the Appeal, we were already able to adjust the 'amount raised' figure upwards to £7,000. This letter, which became known as the 'Mayday!' letter, was dated 9 May. It ended: 'But whatever you can afford, please send it quickly. This could be a now-or-never opportunity as far as securing *Nancy*'s future is concerned.'

The donations began rolling in. A New Zealand TAR, Peter Dowden, put the appeal onto a Ransome user group on the internet, and support began to come from around the world—notably America, the Antipodes, Japan. Particularly Japan, which for some reason has a particular affinity with the Ransome books, and their settings, and which had its own Arthur Ransome Club a good while before TARS was founded. Japanese supporters are often extremely thoughtful, in imaginative ways. One contributor went to immense trouble with exchange rates in order that her donation might amount to exactly £525, the amount Ransome himself originally paid for *Nancy*.

At one stage I began, rather half-heartedly, to send appeals to well-known individuals who I thought might support us. As a result, I have a letter from the secretary of Sir Edward Heath, politely declining on Sir Edward's behalf, and a short, but rather splendid one from Terry Pratchett, in which he describes himself as 'negatively enthusiastic' about *Swallows and Amazons*, and adds that he plans to save his money 'in case *Just William*'s house comes on the market.'

In reality, our best hope was our core constituency of known Ransome fans, and they weren't letting us down. Cheques arrived with every post and I began to believe we might make it. I hoped so, because if we didn't there was no Plan B.

One disappointment was that the few letters of active discouragement came from people whom I respected and in some cases admired as experienced sailors who knew what they were talking about. They argued cogently why it would never work, and in some cases seemed to have got into cahoots (they were nearly all from the East Coast and undoubtedly knew each other) to sing from the same hymn sheet of RYA orthodoxy. One, to my disappointment, was Greg Palmer, by then based in St Petersburg, where he had sailed, in *Peter Duck*, to help realise the building of the replica of Peter the Great's flagship the *Shtandart*. Although, having dutifully talked-down the project, he ended cheerfully, 'If however you ignore this advice as I suspect you will, you can count on me for help and support.' Unfortunately he died of a heart-attack before I could take him up on this offer.

The time had rolled round for the TARS AGM again, always held across the late May Bank Holiday, this time on the Norfolk Broads, at Horning Hall Farm, in a field beside the River Bure. Around the campsite, and on the excursions (splendid trip on the three pleasure wherries) I met with numerous well-wishers, and not a few who handed over cheques, but deliberately kept to myself the state of the bank balance. I wanted to give myself the pleasure of creating an effect at the meeting. This time I had a slot in the agenda. 'As you know,' I told the members, 'we have been given an imminent deadline to raise £25,000, or risk losing the opportunity to buy *Nancy*. A month ago we had £2,000 in the bank. I can report that as of this morning our funds stand at... £22,500.' The effect was all I could have wished for. Cheers and applause from the floor of the meeting, and among the committee members on the podium some faces expressed delight, some looked thunderstruck. Christina Hardyment, one of the founders of TARS and by then a vice-president, immediately stood up and proposed an annual grant of £2,000 towards maintenance, carried overwhelmingly (though later whittled down to £500).

A few days later, we passed the magic figure—the appeal topped-out at around £30,000, which gave us a useful margin for eventualities—and we completed the purchase of *Nancy* on 9 June.

The Appeal had become a 'company limited by guarantee'—the Nancy Blackett Trust Limited—a few days earlier, on 28 May, though its charitable status took a little longer. The Charity Commissioners required evidence of *Nancy Blackett*'s ability to 'confer a benefit on a significant section of the public' and that she was of 'architectural, historic or educational merit'. The best way of obtaining this, I thought, was to ask suitably authoritative figures for statements in support of her significance, a request which resulted in glowing, and moving testimonials.

Dr Roger Knight, then deputy director of the National Maritime Museum, wrote '*Nancy Blackett* is the most evocative and tangible link with the author Arthur Ransome... Ransome's books have influenced the children of several generations, imbuing a significant section of them with a love of the sea which has been translated into active sailing and care for an important part of our heritage and environment. The most important underlying goal of the Trust is to widen that understanding by making *Nancy Blackett* accessible to a wider public.'

Christina Hardyment described *Nancy* as 'one of the best loved little ships in Britain, an inspiration to generations of children who learnt the value of courage and high endeavours from reading Arthur Ransome's books.' Of *We Didn't Mean to Go to Sea*, she said, 'Literary critics regard this tense, thrilling novel as the high point of Ransome's writing. No decent cabin library is without it.'

Peter Hunt, professor of children's literature at the University of Wales, and author of *Approaching Arthur Ransome*, pointed out the 'cultural importance of children's literature', and Arthur Ransome's central position within it— 'undoubtedly one of the five most important writers for children of the twentieth century.' *We Didn't Mean to Go to Sea*, 'probably his masterpiece', is 'a classic of sailing literature as well as children's literature. The preservation of the actual vessel would seem to be of valid historic importance. In educational terms the *Nancy Blackett* has great potential'.

Though this proved enough to convince the Charity Commissioners of the worth of the project in general, they remained unpersuaded that the preservation of a mere boat—however self-evidently significant we might regard it—was a sufficiently charitable objective in itself. Accordingly, and with advice from the NCVO, we recast the Trust's objects as 'to advance the education and understanding of the public in the works of Arthur Ransome', but with the principal means of doing so, the purchase and maintenance of the *Nancy Blackett*, relegated to one of the 'powers'. This worked, so by the middle of 1997, just a little over a year after the idea had first been conceived, we had purchased *Nancy*, and had put in place a registered charity to look after her. Now all we had to do was work out what we were going to do with her.

CHAPTER TEN

'She's beginning something already'

❧

Owning a boat is a very different matter from wanting, or planning to own one. Put like that, it seems obvious, but the change of gear is dramatic, especially when the boat is the *Nancy Blackett*. She entered our lives, like her fictional, human namesake, seemingly with a brisk agenda of her own.

Long before the appeal had gone into overdrive, we had learned that Ipswich was to hold a Maritime Festival in the summer of 1997, and we had arranged with Colin that, whether he or we owned *Nancy* at the time, she would be there—it would be a valuable publicity opportunity. But when we completed the purchase, the date of the festival was less than three weeks away; no work had been done on *Nancy* over the winter, and she was still high and dry, chocked-up in Harbour Marine's yard at Southwold. Mercifully, she was in pretty good shape, though our pre-purchase survey has thrown up a handful of immediate requirements. John Buckley and his team at Harbour Marine made a superhuman effort to get her ready, and in the water, in time, and even provided a couple of their staff to sail her round.

Meanwhile, by one of those strange coincidences, the BBC has taken it into its head to do an item for its *Bookworm* programme on Ransome's East Coast books, and, about a week before the festival, rang to ask if they could use *Nancy* to do some filming. Happily we were able to say yes, and arranged for it to take place immediately after the festival finished.

Now is probably a good time to introduce one or two of the other participants in the Trust. Terry Absalom had written to me early on, a letter full of enthusiasm, including the all-important offer to get stuck in and help. Terry was physically very strong, immensely sociable and came with a built-in can-do attitude, a great sense of humour and a wealth of amusing anecdotes. More importantly, he was a capable and experienced sailor (he'd taken part in the Sydney-Hobart race), and had owned and restored several classic cars, which meant he had experience in overseeing restoration work by professional craftsmen. He was just what *Nancy* and the Trust needed. Terry was an airline pilot with British Midland, working short-haul flights—his rosters always seemed flexible enough to give him time for *Nancy* when needed.

Terry's was one of the three names on the original company document of incorporation—the other, apart from mine, was Bill Oatey, who again had volunteered out of the blue. Bill owned a 24ft gaff cutter, a Norfolk Gypsy, and as it happened also had a background in civil aviation—he was a retired safety officer at Heathrow Airport. Bill, steady and grounded, and Terry, well, flighty, made an excellent combination on the slowly-developing board of the trust.

For Ipswich, Terry and I decided we should have a stand there, in addition to *Nancy* herself, to sell Ransome books, the videos, badges (I'd had some made up, incorporating the phrase 'Grab a chance and you won't be sorry for a might-have-been'), publicise the presence of *Nancy* and recruit new members. We booked a last-minute site, alongside the magnificent Custom House, but, with a few days to go, had nothing to build the stand out of. Terry, ever resourceful in such situations, borrowed an impressively battered Transit minibus from his local scout troop, and some scaffolding poles and a disreputable blue tarpaulin from a builder friend. The length of some of the poles dictated that the size of our stand was way over our allocated area, but luckily no-one seemed to mind, or maybe notice. The tarpaulin proved to be ancient and cracked, and what was worse, covered with remnants of cement. This meant that if it did rain, it would let in not only water, but dirty water at that, onto our precious stock. We hastily obtained some clear plastic sheeting, ready for any emergencies, but mercifully the weather stayed fine.

With another NBT trustee, Brian Hammett, multi-tasking officer of the Cruising Association and President of the East Coast Old Gaffers, providing the running commentary on the festival's Tannoy, there was little chance that *Nancy* would be overlooked, and we acquired many new friends and members. We also had a visit from the local radio station, doing a live interview—which resulted twenty minutes later in a woman rushing up to the stand, saying 'I heard you in the car—where is she?'.

On the Saturday, my wife Wendy arrived with our two daughters, Eleanor and Paula, then aged 13 and 10. They were keen Ransome fans, especially Eleanor who had read all the books at least twice and had a habit of winning quizzes at TARS AGMs. This was the first time they'd seen *Nancy*; we were to sleep aboard, and they were thrilled, and slightly awed at the prospect (as, to be honest, was I, and still am). We'd just got ourselves bedded-down, the girls up for'ard, myself in John's bunk, and turned down the paraffin cabin lamps when the cabin door crashed open, and a torch flashed in. It was Harbour Marine's owner John Buckley, who was on another boat rafted up just behind us. They were keeping an eye on *Nancy* for us, but we, unaware of this, hadn't told them she would be occupied that night.

Immediately the festival closed, on the Sunday, we dropped *Nancy* down the river to meet up with the BBC at Woolverstone Marina. A gratifyingly large number of extra children appeared, courtesy of TARS member Dave Sewart who had been camping with them nearby, and they began to clamber enthusiastically and photogenically over the foredeck while I stood in front and did a short piece to camera about the Trust. The following day, two of them, Andrew and Emily Weeks, were selected to play John and Susan, and haul (rather unconvincingly) on ropes, and peer nervously out of portholes—with more conviction, some suitably atrocious weather having turned up for the sailing sequences—ready to have passages from *We Didn't Mean to Go to Sea* read over the top of them in the final edit.

Griff Rhys Jones, who hosted the programme and as a Ransome fan himself had initiated the project, turned up. There was also an actor who played Ransome, and spoke his words—he had a rich, fruity voice just like everyone imagines, wrongly, Ransome to have had. In fact his radio voice was rather light and restrained, not unlike that of Richard Briers. But the fruity voice worked on this occasion.

There was also a script-girl, who at one stage staggered out of the cabin, looking rather green, and bumped into Terry Absalom. 'Have you been smoking down there?' she asked, accusingly. Terry said that nobody had, we didn't allow it, and asked why. 'Because there's this strong smell of pipe-tobacco,' she replied. It called to mind the story told by previous owners, Bill and Eunice Bentley, to Christina Hardyment, that they would occasionally smell an unaccountable whiff

Young visitors make themselves at home on the foredeck, 1997

NBT members' winter working party, February 1998

of pipe-smoke about the cabin. Perhaps the ghost of Ransome was puffing his approval, and enjoyment, once again.

Later in the summer, Terry, Martin and I took *Nancy* down to another maritime festival, at Chatham. Although this one was less successful, being the victim of poor weather and feeble publicity, at least we had a proper tented stand this time, and our takings were pretty much in line with Ipswich. We also made some new friends: one of our neighbours was marine artist Claudia Myatt, who became a staunch supporter. She did a painting of *Nancy* and has gone on to design numerous greeting cards, teatowels, mugs and other items that have helped raise funds. And we found our next treasurer, and now webmaster, Irwin Jacobson, there.

Just a week after Chatham, on Sunday 31 August, we'd arranged for *Nancy* to be 'at home' for members to come and see her for themselves at her base in Woolverstone Marina. Terry arrived the previous night, got up early and dressed her overall with every flag, pennant and bit of bunting he could find. He'd just finished, at about 8 o'clock in the morning, with *Nancy* a riot of cheerful colour when someone walked past, looked askance at the decorations, and said, 'You haven't heard then.'

This was the morning that the country was waking up to the news that Princess Diana had been killed. Down came the bunting, and we wondered briefly whether it would be right to cancel the whole event. But many members had booked for the day, and nearly all arrived. It was the first chance we'd had of offering the members the chance of a sail on *Nancy*, and the weather was perfect. Nearly fifty people enjoyed short trips down to Pin Mill and back, and later on, a barbecue.

Autumn came, and it was time to think about taking *Nancy* out of the water and getting some work done on her. The pre-purchase survey, undertaken by the very knowledgeable Peter Brown (who sadly died shortly afterwards) had identified a number of areas of rot, some of which boatbuilder John Buckley, who had been working on her for years, refused to believe were there, until he looked for himself. We'd considered the merits of getting competitive quotes for the work, but having assured ourselves that Harbour Marine's rates were fair, concluded that the benefits of having *Nancy* looked after by people who knew and understood her (particularly at this early stage in our own acquaintance with her) out-weighed possible gains from taking her elsewhere.

Accordingly, one day in early October, Terry and I set off down the Orwell to sail *Nancy* back to her winter quarters in Southwold. It was my first opportunity to find out what *Nancy* was really like under sail—all my trips so far had been short boat movements under engine. Today, we had a perfect beam wind, once we got out to sea, a brisk force four or five, enough to justify throwing a reef in. Even so, she picked up her skirts and, well heeled-over, fairly flew along, clocking well over seven knots over the ground at times.

So fast was our passage that we managed to get the tides all wrong for the notoriously tricky Southwold harbour entrance. We gunned the engine and went for it, but got caught in a fast eddy that seemed determined to sweep us, bowsprit first, into the north wall. I think the sheer horror of the situation caused me to black out for a moment. When I came to, the engine was at full throttle in reverse, and Terry was backing us safely out of the maelstrom. We took another, more calculated shot at it, and managed to get in, grateful to see John on the harbour wall to guide us up the river.

Even so, we managed to touch the putty on the hump in the middle, but the tide was on the rise, and we were soon off.

That winter saw a good deal of skilled surgery by the yard. Sufficient work needed doing to justify our taking the hull back to bare wood. It included replacing the stem, which had had piecemeal repairs, with a single, laminated, length of wood. We also decided to spline the hull—replace the caulking between the planks with glued-in strips of pitch pine which would stiffen her a lot, and also increase watertightness.

There was also a lot of less-skilled work to be done, and come February we arranged two successive, and successful, weekend working parties which enabled members to get their hands on *Nancy*, and feel they were doing something—as they were—to both look after her, and conserve the funds of the trust. About thirty members took part in all. Even though the weekends, both the work itself and the after-work socialising, were very enjoyable, we never quite replicated their success in later years. We were warned that enthusiasm would drop off, and so, in this respect it did, though not ruinously.

We still have a group of members who are glad to assist, particularly at laying-up and refitting times—antifouling is a suitable and, when the weather is kind, surprisingly popular task—or who offer to undertake specific projects. But in general, letting the yard get on with things seems the more efficient option. It also means *Nancy* is cared for by skilled craftsmen, and nowhere is this more true than in her varnishing. We concluded early on that we owe it to her and her heritage status to give her the best possible care. I'd certainly counsel any other organisation which was counting on volunteer labour to think very carefully.

But by the end of that winter—our first lay-up season with *Nancy*—we felt that, not only did we at last truly own her, but also that she was ready for anything.

CHAPTER ELEVEN

Down-Channel

❧

Highlight of the following season, 1998, was *Nancy*'s voyage to Falmouth and back. Why Falmouth? Well, right at the beginning of *We Didn't Mean to Go to Sea*, just after the Swallows have met Jim Brading, and been invited aboard the *Goblin*, John asks Jim: 'What's the furthest you've ever been in her?'

Jim's reply—'Uncle Bob and I took her down to Falmouth and back one year'—opens up a link between them. 'We used to sail there with Daddy when he was on leave,' John tells him, and then adds: 'But only in an open boat. We never had one we could sleep in.' This is the cue—and one has to admire the breathtaking speed and economy with which Ransome achieves this—for Jim to issue his invitation to 'spend a night in the *Goblin*' and so get the whole adventure started.

Falmouth then is a pretty significant place—the learning to sail with Daddy has already been mentioned in *Swallows and Amazons*, as well as in *Swallowdale* and *Peter Duck*. Ransome himself had spent some happy times in the area. In November 1933, just after the publication of *Winter Holiday*, he and Evgenia went down there (by steamship) and stayed in the Watch House at St Mawes, just across the harbour from Falmouth itself. (He paid tribute to St Mawes some years, and books, later in the postscript to *Missee Lee*, when the junk *Shining Moon* ends up anchored off its harbour mouth.) It is very likely that it was there that he conceived the desire to own an offshore boat which led to the move to East Anglia and the purchase of *Nancy*. So it seemed a very appropriate object for our first long voyage with *Nancy*. Not only a good shake-down cruise, but also one which would cover a good deal of coast, enabling *Nancy* to be seen by many of the people who had subscribed to her purchase. Furthermore, it fitted well with another major engagement: the first International Festival of the Sea to take place at Portsmouth.

Thus it was that, after another Ipswich Festival, and our own first AGM, held at the Royal Harwich Yacht Club in Woolverstone, and a photocall with East Coast boat photographer Den Phillips for a *Yachting Monthly* feature, *Nancy* headed south across the Thames Estuary, and down-Channel.

We'd received various invitations to call in on our way along the coast—one we couldn't refuse was to visit a TARS weekend camp at Cobnor in Chichester Harbour, organised by the Southern region. *Nancy* anchored in Bosham Creek, a dory had been loaned by a nearby sailing school to ferry people out, and soon the cockpit and cabin-top was a mass of children, and grown-ups. Roger Wardale was on hand with his Leica, and his fine photo of *Nancy* under sail appeared a year later on the dust-jacket of *Ransome on Blue Water Sailing*, a collection of his writings subscription-published by Amazon Publications, an offshoot of TARS.

By this time we had begun to recruit some able volunteer skippers. One of them, Peter Randall, a professional Yachtmaster instructor, was off Poole Harbour, en route from Lymington to Weymouth under engine when it began misfiring, and eventually died altogether. A local angling club took her in tow, dropping her off at the Town Quay. Peter repaid them with all the beer that was on board (not much) and set to diagnosing the fault. Symptoms suggested a fuel blockage, but the problem turned out to be a failed lift pump. A replacement needed to be ordered, which would take a few days to arrive. No doubt *Nancy* enjoyed being back in the harbour where Ransome had discovered her (in fact she scarcely seems able to pass the place without developing some sort of ailment as an excuse to linger there) but it was frustrating for the crew. Between them they jury-rigged a gravity-feed system for the diesel, which perhaps predictably failed when *Nancy* heeled on the 'wrong' tack, but enabled her to limp round to Cobb's Quay Marina. Then they went home, while *Nancy* awaited the replacement pump.

This unscheduled stopover meant *Nancy* missing the Plymouth Classics weekend, but having arranged to take the bookstall and exhibition down, I went anyway, and contrived to call into Poole on my way home, just to see *Nancy*, really, and nominally to check that all was well with the now-all-but-fixed fuel pump. It also provided a chance to grab a quick drink with the oncoming skipper. This was Steve le Butt, and we managed to arrive at the marina, from opposite directions, at about the same time—around eight o'clock on a dreary, misty evening. Steve

taught biology, and sailing, at King Edward's School near Godalming, where one
of our trustees, Rodney Fox, was headmaster. He'd already helped out with the
dory at Cobnor, and was now to take *Nancy* all the way to Falmouth, and part of
the way back.

Steve brought his girlfriend Claire, another teacher, with him, as part of the
crew for the first leg. Less experienced, or more cautious than Steve, she was
warning him against the folly of prancing about on a bouncy deck—except that,
with her gloriously rich Northern Ireland accent, it came out more as 'Proincing
aboit on a boincy deck', delivered in a lilt that was itself so boincy that Steve and I
fell about laughing, and the phrase has become one of the NBT and Willis family
sayings.

The third member of the crew was to join the following morning, so I didn't
meet him then. In his log of the voyage, written-up for *Jibbooms and Bobstays*,
the Trust's newsletter, he introduces himself in the third person (appropriately
enough, I suppose).

> Tuesday 4 August: Cobb's Quay Marina, Poole, not far from where AR collected
> *Nancy Blackett* for the first time in 1935. The wet weather of the past week has
> cleared and *Nancy*'s fuel pump is just about ready. Skipper Steve and his new crew,
> Claire and Roger, begin to get to know one another and stores are stowed as we
> wait for the 1430 bridge opening. There's some hard driving if we are to make Fal-
> mouth for the Classic Boats at the weekend, but a bridge is a bridge, and sailors
> must be patient.

After rejecting the options of a night passage—crew too new—and Weymouth—
ETA well after midnight—they decided to duck into Lulworth Cove. Roger again:

> At night the cliff at the back of the cove merges into the cliffs either side; as we
> nosed carefully towards the shore it seemed impossible to tell where the narrow
> opening lay. (No leading lights!) Without GPS it would have been unthinkable.
> The skipper was on the point of aborting and heading for Weymouth when we saw
> the anchor lights of the yachts already in the cove and sought a safe anchorage in
> the dim moonlight. Lying at anchor, heading a light NW wind exposed us abeam to

a SW swell which kept *Nancy* rolling until the wind backed and died in the morning; the price of our audacity.

Round Portland Bill, close to slack water, inside the overfalls and across Lyme Bay—'some good sailing but the promised NW wind proved elusive and the tide was setting us well into the bay... The last four hours into Brixham has to be with the help of the sturdy donkey.' Then a lunch stop at Dartmouth, overnights at Salcombe and Fowey, and so to Saturday. 'Another fine day and an early start. A pleasant reach to SW brought us to Falmouth Roads in the late morning. Classic boats all around us caused great excitement.'

Ashore meanwhile, the Willis family had driven down to Falmouth, and set up camp on a rather posh site down at Maen Valley, and made contact with another TARS family, the Osborns, who were camping at an altogether more funky cheese-making farm overlooking the Helford River. The previous evening I'd found the HQ of Falmouth Classics, being organised that year by our good friend Aidan de la Mare, but Aidan wasn't around, and being without a boat I'd felt rather out of things. So I was delighted to observe *Nancy* sailing in, and watch her finding a berth, and was looking forward to meeting 'my' crew.

We arranged, via my newly-acquired mobile phone, to meet up outside the Chain Locker pub on the Town Quay. Identification threatened to be an issue, as I'd not met this Roger, but Eleanor's bright red, self-knitted Amazon hat helped a great deal, and soon Roger Sturge and I were getting acquainted over a pint. It was a more significant meeting than perhaps either of us was aware of at the time.

Roger, a retired educationalist from an old Bristol Quaker family was a TARS member, but not one given to joining in meetings and activities. He had actually met Arthur Ransome, though remembered little of it, being about two at the time. Ransome, who knew his parents, dubbed him 'the complete Dutchman' in honour of his romper suit, which, just like the Dutch menswear seen by the Swallows in Flushing, featured 'wide baggy trousers that came in at the ankles'. Roger was full of enthusiasm for *Nancy*, her significance and her possibilities, and needed little persuading to join the board; he has at various times filled the roles of sailing secretary, treasurer and company secretary, usually at least two at once. In 2013 he took over the position of chairman.

After lunch it was decided that Steve and Roger would take Diana Osborn with some of the children, Eleanor and the Osborn boys Felix and Barnaby, for a sail round to the Helford River, and the rest of us would drive round and meet them there. Which is what we did, making our way to Durgan beach in time to see *Nancy* round up under main and let go the anchor, at the most westerly point of her voyage westward, and indeed the farthest west she has been with the Trust, or possibly ever. The anchor was her old fisherman's anchor, and is clearly visible, along with Diana being rowed ashore by Eleanor in the inflatable, in one of my all-time favourite photos of *Nancy*.

We seemed to have got our wires crossed with the Classics however. While we were up the Helford, they were in Carrick Roads, and the next morning, when I joined to crew to explore Carrick Roads, they were off to Helford Passage. No matter, we were happy to be simply enjoying *Nancy* in this splendid sailing area, and had a spiffing sail, up almost as far as the King Harry Ferry and across to St Mawes.

In the evening, another new crew member made the mobile-assisted introduction outside the Chain Locker. This was Sheila Campbell, who arrived, driven down by her then non-sailing husband John, bearing a ready-roasted chicken with which to feed the crew on the return trip. Sheila also got bitten by the *Nancy* bug and eventually became membership secretary.

Nancy's first major port of call on the return trip was Teignmouth, at the invitation of a clutch of TARS who lived there. It's a tricky harbour to get into, but our hosts had prepared a fine welcome, with not only a reserved space on the harbour wall, but also a display in the window of the local bookshop and, later, a reception in the yacht club. Brigit Sanders, TARS life-president, our patron and the original of the 'ship's baby' Bridget in *We Didn't Mean to Go to Sea* ('A faint grunt came from the fore-cabin where Bridget had curled herself up in Titty's bunk and was pretending to be asleep. 'No, no, no,' said Mother. 'No stowaways…'') drove over from her home in Bideford. It was the first time she'd seen *Nancy* since the Butt and Oyster dinner in 1989, and she pronounced her, 'Quite 'all Sir Garnet'', to the pleasure of everyone who understood the phrase (it's an east-coast term meaning neatly and correctly turned-out). She was also impressed by the number of children swarming over *Nancy*, polishing the portholes with Brasso-soaked cloths.

And then, a few up-Channel hops later, it was time for Portsmouth, and the International Festival of the Sea.

Portsmouth. I'd done precious little sailing on this epic voyage, apart mainly from one glorious day-trip dash down the Solent all the way from Northney Marina at the top of Chichester Harbour to Lymington, and the pottering about at Falmouth. I had a living to earn, a largely non-sailing family to spend time with and no shortage of *Nancy*-related paperwork to keep me occupied. In any case, at an early stage in the proceedings, I'd set the bar for skipper qualifications at a level appropriate to *Nancy*'s value and her activities, but which I, with my shore-based Yachtmaster, taken three times over the years but never matched with the practical certificate, fell well short of. So I wasn't complaining—though I occasionally felt a little envious when I'd receive a phone-call from the crew reporting in from, for example, 'the best fish restaurant in Brixham'. But I had no intention of missing this one.

Portsmouth Harbour is just about my favourite place in the world, historic, dramatic, endlessly alive and exciting, and down in Old Portsmouth, at Point, one can watch the comings and goings through the narrow entrance, with fishing boats—and car ferries, and the occasional yacht—bearing round to the right, into the Camber dock. Most of the yachts head further up the harbour, or over to the Gosport marinas on the far side. The odd naval vessel will be heading for the dockyard, straight ahead, and dominated by the masts of HMS *Victory* and the Semaphore Tower atop the redbrick Georgian buildings.

My grandfather had worked in the dockyard and my father, a naval draughtsman, began his career there. (He eventually transferred to the Admiralty in London, his office being middle window, on the second floor above the middle arch of Admiralty Arch. Or so my mother would have us children believe.) He was a member of Portsmouth Sailing Club, also on Point, back along Bath Square in its tall, gabled former consulate HQ. My first-ever sail was in one of the Victory class keelboats specific to the harbour, belonging to a friend of his. And it recently came to light that my 19th-century ancestor, one Joseph Procter, was the Portsmouth Harbourmaster (probably meaning the Camber basin), and lived in Bath Square. When it comes to scattering my ashes, there'll be a good pinch for the Orwell, of course (it's already claimed my first wedding ring) and perhaps for

Falmouth too, but I'd want the bulk of them to be wafted by the breeze across the waters of Portsmouth Harbour.

And now, here I was about to enter it aboard *Nancy Blackett*. The crew was the old firm, Terry and me, augmented on this occasion by Christina Hardyment. Christina had written an article on *Nancy* for *Country Life*, and contrived to have it published this same week. Thus she was able to inform her readers that 'as you read this I shall be helming *Nancy Blackett* into Portsmouth Harbour for the Festival of the Sea.' We marvelled at the predictability of life in the countryside, which ensured that all those stately-home owners and parents of those carefully-photographed daughters would have simultaneously reached the relevant page by coffee-time on the day of publication—but we ensured that Christina had hold of the tiller, just in case anyone should be watching.

I, meanwhile, was drinking in the view as we went through the narrows—the Square Tower, then the Round Tower and next to it the distinctive turreted Tower House, home of the great marine artist W. L. Wyllie, who had had a hand in founding the sailing club, then the crenellated ramparts of the waterside house of Harry Brickwood, brewer and yachtsman, the boomyard, where my dad had kept his little sailing dinghy *Dabchick*, the sailing club itself, the Still and West pub, before the harbour opened out to reveal the magnificent tall ship, the *Sedov*, her sails loosely furled, against the dockyard wall. Our spirits, already high, lifted another notch. This, the first festival of its kind in this famous old dockyard, was going to be some-thing very special and we, *Nancy* and the Trust, were going to be part of it.

We made our way into Basin 2, along with about 300 other classic and tra-ditional yachts, fishing boats and motor cruisers. Fortunately we were ahead of most of them, and were directed to a berth alongside the pontoon on the western side of the dock. Since the boats ended up rafted-out six or seven deep, this was just as well, as we were expecting visitors. *Nancy*'s presence had been well-pub-licised in our own and TARS' newsletters, and in addition we had a stall in the Heritage Afloat marquee, from which we could direct visitors. Even so we were unprepared for the huge level of interest. *Nancy*'s cabin seemed to be continu-ously occupied with visitors with the cockpit, and sometimes the pontoon as well, acting as a holding area. Often they would be family parties, with maybe three generations, of grandparents, parents and kids, who had been brought up on, or

Farthest West (we think): *Nancy Blackett* drops anchor in the Helford River

Nancy Blackett (foreground) and *Coch-y-bonddhu* on the Walton Backwaters

were now being introduced to, *Swallows and Amazons*. The youngsters were wide-eyed, and delighted in clambering out of the fore-hatch and rushing along the deck, while their seniors were more misty-eyed, and preferred just to sit and soak up the atmosphere of the cabin. For us, it was a constant thrill, and a reward for all our efforts, to watch the emotions on their faces as they stepped, not only onto Ransome's own boat, but right into the pages of one of his best books.

In all we estimate we entertained over 800 people aboard *Nancy* over the four days of the festival—not bad considering that, as we eventually discovered, the basin and its pontoons were supposed to be off-limits to the general public. In theory, *Nancy* was not one of the show-attractions, like the Tall Ships, the *Matthew*, or the aircraft carriers which visitors were allowed aboard. We were there, we found, along with all the other boats in Basin 2, to provide a background 'forest of masts'—just one among hundreds of small boats whose owners had applied to bring them to the festival, and which had been chosen for their traditional style and good looks. They were there to be lived-aboard, but not to be visited.

In fact the restriction was not enforced at all, other than by small notices at the tops of the ramps leading down to the pontoons. And we couldn't have been busier, if there had been neon signs pointing to *Nancy*. Eleanor and her TARS friend Lucy, who lived in Portsmouth (and whose parents provided us with welcome hot baths and beds) sold hundreds of raffle tickets, occasionally pausing to give improptu penny-whistle concerts in the cockpit, and we met dozens of old, and new members. One of the pleasures of the festival, for me, was seeing *Peter Duck*, another of Ransome's boats, back from her sojourn in St Petersburg (sadly without Greg Palmer aboard; he had died out there from a heart attack the previous year); another was a friendly handshake from Richard Woodman, who had officiated at the 'Great Race' between *Nancy* and *Peter Duck* back in 1994, but who had been among those expressing reservations when the idea of the Trust was originally proposed. His *Andromeda* was rafted-up a few boats outside us.

I seemed to spend my time running between the boat and the bookstall (they were about a quarter of a mile apart) and didn't even manage to buy a T-shirt with *Nancy*'s name among the list of boats on the back until the end of the last day. The one non-*Nancy* memory I do have, is of a French theatre company using (to its fullest extent—spars and all) an old sailing barge to perform an adaptation of

Lewis Carroll's *The Hunting of the Snark*. It provided another useful phrase or saying for maritime occasions: *Your sheep weel be so to speak Snarrked.*

Our sheep, sorry, ship, was indeed soon to be snarked. Our plan, on coming out of Portsmouth, had been to sail *Nancy* straight up to Scarborough, but adverse weather pinned her in the Channel and it was not to be. Probably it was an over-ambitious goal anyway, but TARS Northern region had organised a trip to the town, which has other Ransome associations—his parents met on the beach, and it was in the Spa Pavilion in 1937 that he was presented with the first-ever Carnegie Medal, in honour of *Pigeon Post*. It had seemed a good opportunity for *Nancy* to revisit the harbour from which she had been rescued some ten years previously, and to meet some more of her supporters. We also persuaded Mike Rines to come and give a lunchtime talk on the restoration at the Scarbourough Yacht Club, which inhabits an old lighthouse on the end of the harbour pier.

In the event, I drove up, and so did Mike. Walking along the promenade in the morning, I'd noticed a little yacht, some way offshore, fighting her way towards the harbour. My first reaction had been how much like *Nancy* she looked, followed by the wild hope that maybe the guys had made a superhuman effort and got her up here after all. They would have also had to, for some reason, changed her sails—these were white—and her rig, to gaff. And, on reflection, she seemed a good deal smaller, perhaps 24ft. Even so, she was a cheering sight, and I took her as a good omen. A little while later, I met Mike, rushing breathlessly up the steps of the club. 'I've just seen *Nancy*, coming into the harbour!' he burst out. There was the little white cutter again, her sails furled by now, and I explained how I'd made the same mistake. The odd thing was, though, I met the same boat (wish I could remember her name) three years later at the next Festival of the Sea, and it turned out her bowsprit had originally belonged to *Nancy*.

Mike more than made up for the lack of *Nancy*—he'd brought with him a whole tableful of artefacts rescued from her during the restoration, and as he described how he found her, and patiently negotiated her purchase, we were able to look down through a big picture window at the very spot on the harbour wall where she had been lying at the time. As we left the club, Jim Andrews, another of the early sceptics, came up and pressed me warmly by the hand, leaving a fairly substantial wad of banknotes in it.

So ended *Nancy*'s first full season with the Trust. Some disappointments, but many more reasons to be pleased. She'd sailed at least 1,000 miles, probably more than in any succeeding season, giving around twenty members a chance to crew her, with many others getting short sails, as well as the chance to help out at festivals and the like, and she had been visited by well over 1,000 appreciative Arthur Ransome fans.

CHAPTER TWELVE

Further Adventures

❦

Following the success of *Nancy*'s 1998 voyage to Falmouth and back, we set to work over the succeeding seasons to replicate and consolidate what we had achieved and learned on that trip. Our main aims were to maintain *Nancy*'s visibility and availability, and to keep her sailing, on the grounds that the best-preserved boat is one that keeps working and making demands on those responsible for its upkeep. Note how I avoid using the word 'owners'. Yes, legally we had a certificate showing that we, the Trust, owned sixty-four sixty-fourths of the vessel the *Nancy Blackett*, but like many another individual or group paying the bills on a historic vessel, or even just an 'old boat', we regarded ourselves, and still do, as custodians rather than proprietors.

We had seen all too often how boats which remained static, perhaps in museums, accumulated problems of deterioration which, all too often, could be ignored, while whatever budget there was (never enough, in all probability) might be siphoned off to meet any number of competing demands, for marketing, administration, or whatever, meaning that work on the fabric of the boat was postponed, sometimes beyond the point of no, or impossibly expensive, return. Our gut feeling was that as long as we kept *Nancy* sailing, we'd keep her alive. We'd already seen what a few years of idleness and neglect would do to her.

We did however devote a lot of thought to the question of *Nancy*'s authenticity. The whole issue of boat preservation is fraught with argument about how best to maintain this against, for an active boat, the often competing grounds of safety and practicality. Boats can be regarded as 'restorations' with little more 'original' timber than the keel—or even less—and even that may have been subject to renewal back in the mists of time. The fact of the matter is that pretty well every bit of a wooden boat is built to be expendable, and replaceable, as dictated by the ravages of time, ill-treatment or accident. It's the 'old knife' principle—still the original despite three new blades and five new handles. *Nancy*'s fabric we knew was a great deal more authentic than that, but this did not prevent us from taking a 'robust' rather than a 'purist' attitude to maintenance, repair and, on occasion, equipment. On the other hand, nor did it stop us from making the most of 'authentic' bits of her, notably the nails recovered from her planking, which could be sold, nicely mounted with a certificate, for £10 a time (there are still a few left). We winced a little at the previous owner's new companionway doors, and our purist sides regretted the fact that he'd made cockpit self-draining, rather than keeping the original deep Hillyard design, but we were quietly relieved that this decision, with its practical safety implications, had been taken for us.

Yet we agonised over the issue of stanchions and guard rails. If *Nancy* were ever to stand a chance of being 'coded-in'—ie meeting the MCA's *Code of Practice* for charter vessels—she would need them. But installing them would irrevocably alter her appearance and destroy an important aspect of her character—rather ironically it was the very lack of guard rails that had contributed to John's 'almost OB' accident on *Goblin*'s foredeck, which now constituted an argument against installing them on *Nancy*. In the end, we discovered that by opting for club boat status, in effect co-ownership rather than commercial charter, we could sail *Nancy* within a much less restrictive regime. It's more than likely that *Nancy* was in any case unfitted for ever meeting the requirements of modern charter standards, but we did not feel that this absolved us from meeting such safety requirements as were consistent with her age and status. We compensated where we could, for example with jackstays rather than guardrails—but we had found a 'middle way' of preserving both her heritage value and the well-being of those who sailed in her.

Underlying all our efforts was the simple aim of bringing Ransome's sailing, and his books, to life. For our next season, 1999, we decided to focus on his home area, and the sailing grounds he discovered and loved in *Nancy*—Pin Mill, the River Orwell, Harwich Harbour and 'Secret Water' itself, the delightful Walton Backwaters. Having elected to do this, we received an unexpected bonus—the opportunity to reunite *Nancy* with her original tender, Ransome's old dinghy. *Coch-y-bonddhu*.

Cocky, as everyone calls her, appears briefly in one of the books, *The Picts and the Martyrs*, as the *Scarab*, the dinghy built for Dick and Dorothea, but her greater claim to distinction is that of all Ransome's boats, she was the one he clung onto longest—twenty years. He had her built originally for use in the Lakes, and had brought her with him when he moved to the East Coast. He'd quickly discovered that at thirteen feet she was a bit too big to be a proper tender to *Nancy*, and had had another built (the modestly-named *Queen Mary*, probably the original of the *Goblin*'s *Imp*), but he loved sailing *Cocky*. He'd use her to cross between Levington and Pin Mill—much quicker and more pleasant than taking the car through Ipswich—and would often tow her behind *Nancy*, round to the Backwaters, where he would anchor up, and yield to the temptation to take *Cocky* for a sail when he was supposed to be working.

Like *Nancy* and *Amazon*, *Cocky* had been found in a sad condition and restored. She lived at the time in the Windermere Steam Boat Museum, but was allowed out for the occasional sail. I was allowed to collect her after the TARS AGM at Rudyard Lake in Staffordshire, and tow her south. The Trust, through Brian Hammett, had joined the Old Gaffers, and we had entered *Nancy* for their East Coast Classics, an annual round of cruises and races, which included one event of special interest to us. This was the Swallows and Amazons Dinghy Race in the Walton Backwaters, round *Secret Water*'s Swallow Island (known to the Natives as Horsey Island).

This, we decided, should be *Cocky*'s East Coast debut. Unfortunately, however, I totally misjudged the time it would take to trail her from her interim home in Cambridge (bigger than you'd think, East Anglia) and arrived at the launch ramp at Titchmarsh Marina with less than ten minutes to go before the race. Since the start line, at Stone Point, was a good mile or more away, there was obviously no way that *Cocky* and I were going to make it. There was also the matter of the rigging, at present a bundle of miscellaneous spars, ropes and canvas. Even a simple lug rig like *Cocky*'s can take a bit of working out if you're unfamiliar with it. I decided I'd take it slowly. I got the mast up, and after a couple of false starts, had the single lug sail hoisted and ready to cast off. The wind was blowing straight across the marina berth in which we were moored, perfect for a beam reach out of the pontoons and down the little creek into the open Twizzle.

I jumped in and cast off. At this point, as they say, I must have lost my presence of mind, for I decided to take a quick look at my 'chart' (actually Ordnance

Survey map No 169). I looked up, seconds later, as we bumped gently against the hull of a boat moored to the opposite pontoon. I felt extremely dufferish, and relieved no-one was around to see me. Nothing for it but to get the sail down, claw my way along to the end of the row, and try again, this time without mishap.

At last I was sailing *Cocky*—Arthur Ransome's *Coch-y-bonddhu*. Sailing and skippering her. Like John, at night in the *Goblin*, alone with my boat. There is something about being in command of a vessel—even a small one—which is quite different from any other role or relationship with her—even that of owner, which as chairman of the Trust I've occasionally played aboard *Nancy*.

Cocky, with her red sail and 'the golden flash of newly-varnished wood', as Ransome wrote of *Scarab* in *The Picts and The Martyrs*, looked bewitching, and felt happy to be back in the water. We sailed up on a broad reach towards the leaders of the race, who were just coming into view across the now-flooded Wade, and then tacked back with them towards Stone Point (alias Flint Island), where *Nancy* lay at anchor.

That night, *Cocky* rested once more in another of her old haunts, the stable yard at Broke Hall, close to Mike Rines' bungalow conversion in the grounds thereof. It was *Cocky* that Ransome had been hauling ashore when he first met Josephine and George Russell who lived at the Hall and became regular crew aboard *Nancy*. Eventually, when they began to want a boat of their own, he lent them *Cocky* for a couple of years.

Cocky also featured in our AGM which we held that year in her honour in the lightship clubhouse at Levington—dozens of members sailed in her, under the skilled helmsmanship of Martin Lewis. Among them was one Ted Barnes, who as a boy of 12 had learned to sail in her. He was the son of the headmaster of Arnside, the school to which Ransome had sold *Cocky*. 'Rubbing her down and revarnishing her was my regular winter job,' he told us.

Levington also gave us the excuse to visit Ransome's old home at Broke Farm, now Broke House, at the kind invitation of its owner, the Rev Christopher Courtauld. Chris, who founded the Ocean Youth Club with his yawl *Duet* was a fervent Ransome fan, though he hadn't been aware of the connection when he bought the house. He apologised for the fact that there was no longer much of Ransome about the place, which was true enough, though we could look out from the window of his upstairs study and enjoy the view across the Orwell that he had delighted in.

One more high point from the year. Ipswich Maritime Festival, again. Towards the end of the last afternoon, I'm sitting in *Nancy*'s cabin when a dad and daughter come aboard, by no means the first, that weekend or over the preceding couple of years. She, aged about 11, makes a beeline for Titty's bunk and dives into it. He, an obvious East Coast yachtsman, rather piratical in appearance with smock, beard and dark curly hair, just sits on the cabin steps and gazes around in obvious delight, murmuring things like 'Gosh. Arthur Ransome's *Nancy Blackett*. Wow!' This is Bill Wallace King, one of the most enthusiastic of enthusiasts I've ever known. Within weeks he's helping out with the sailing trips at the AGM, within months, he's been co-opted onto the board, and early the following season he's appointed a *Nancy Blackett* skipper.

But every year has to have its low points as well, and for us, two came close together towards the end. *Nancy* was battered by gales on her pontoon at Woolverstone Marina, ironically just the night before she was due to be moved round to Southwold to be laid-up for the winter. A bow-warp parted and she was pushed by wind and tide onto the pontoon, causing friction wear to her planks—chafing them in a similar manner to some of her Scarborough damage—as well some damage to the transom. Luckily she was still able to sail and set off to Southwold a couple of days later, only to have the engine break down outside the harbour. *Nancy* was towed in by the lifeboat, which was particularly embarrassing for her skipper, who was an RNLI seaworthiness examiner. The remedy proved to be a new gearbox. It was an expensive winter for the Trust—while the engine was out we took the opportunity to upgrade the engine compartment with new insulation and an automatic fire-extinguisher, and fit a new fuel tank, in place of the converted water tank that had been serving.

In November, not many days after the gale damage, Brigit Sanders, our beloved Patron, died after an intensification of the respiratory illness that had dogged her last few years. Despite some frailty, she had remained lively almost to the end, and interested, right up to it. Enthusiasm had been her watchword, backed up a keen and perceptive intelligence and a real interest in people, especially young people. Her vision for TARS and the Nancy Blackett Trust was full of adventure and activity. It has not always proved easy to live up to, but when we came to thinking about an appropriate memorial to her, the most obvious answer was a fund to help young people discover and enjoy sailing.

CHAPTER THIRTEEN

Further Adventures II

୧୬

The following year, 2000, was if anything a more extreme mixture of good and ill. It began well with a gratifying letter from the National Historic Ships Committee, informing us that *Nancy* would qualify for inclusion on the *National Register of Historic Vessels*—if only she were larger, or if the NRHV's criteria were wider. The *Register*, set up in 1995, was restricted to vessels which, as well as having the necessary historic value, met the criteria of being over forty years old, over forty feet in length and built in the British Isles. The committee deliberated long over *Nancy*'s eligibility (the odd exception had been made) but eventually concluded that 'her pedigree and associations qualified her for Certificate in all respects other than her size.' Accordingly, she was put on a 'waiting list' of boats that would be eligible for inclusion on the *Register* if and when its criteria were extended. In itself this constituted a fairly exclusive group—about 100 vessels at the time—but the extension still hasn't happened.

At a more parochial level, we'd been talking to the Old Gaffers Association about their Swallows and Amazons race, which we'd so enjoyed the previous summer They'd decided to detach it from its midweek position in the East Coast Classics, and establish it as a freestanding weekend event. One aim of doing this was to enable more children to take part, and this was very much in line with our own aims of promoting sailing among young people.

We'd been given an eighteen-inch length of *Nancy*'s former mast by Mike Rines, and it occurred to us that this would make a nice, and highly appropriate, trophy for the race. Our only problem then was to find someone who would carve it for us. In the end, we found one of the OGA members, Peter Fletcher, a retired boatbuilder who sailed the East Coast, but who coincidentally lived not ten miles from me in Surrey, in Guildford, literally on the banks of the River Wey—he'd built his own smack yacht, *Sarah Grey*, in his back garden, and launched her from there into the river which ran behind it. Peter warmed to the project, donated his time and produced a beautifully-turned goblet-like item, for which he went on to make a mahogany case, with a drawer in the base to take a card giving a brief history of *Nancy*, the Trust and the Trophy, and a silver plate on the inside of the door to record the winners.

The 'Swamazons Weekend', as the OGA people like to call it, has gone on from strength to strength, with a growing number of boats each year (including *Cocky* again in 2001—she came last) and overnight camping available. The race is normally on the Saturday, as near mid-July as the tides will permit, with a fun event such as a treasure hunt or a picnic on the Sunday. Around fifty boats now regularly take part—we'd like to think due to the attraction of the Nancy Blackett Trophy, but in reality it's simply a jolly good idea encapsulated into a well-run event. We later added an additional prize specifically for junior helms.

It was while a few of us were sailing *Nancy* down to the Backwaters for the 2000 Swamazons that the germ of the idea which produced our next Patron was born. Bill Wallace-King was undergoing his skipper assessment, being administered by one of our Senior Skippers, Lewis Dann. Lew is a medical man turned RYA coach—he looked after the UK's Laser and Optimist international teams—and he happened to mention that he knew Ellen MacArthur very well—he came from the same part of Derbyshire as her family, and in fact had been the anaesthetist at her birth. We all knew of her, and admired her for her round-Britain solo sail in her little Corribee, *Iduna*, but this was before she became really (as in outside yachting circles) famous—she hadn't begun, much less completed, the Vendee Globe at that stage. Lew told us she adored the *Swallows and Amazons* books and would love to sail *Nancy*. The more we thought about this, the more we realised what an excellent role model she would make as an embodiment of the sort of values the Trust was aiming to promote. It was Lew, I think, who pointed out that we had a vacancy for a Patron. We all jumped at the idea, and he offered to e-mail Ellen. At that moment she was aboard *Kingfisher*, within a few hours of winning the 1-STAR single-handed Transatlantic race. Lew contacted her a few days later, while she was sailing back, and got an immediate, and enthusiastic response, in Ellen's inimitable boat-lurch, missed-key typing.

'Hi Lew, What a wonderful opportunity, would truly love to. Let me know when the AGM is—where so you fond the young people to sail her? Very busy, but wanted to reply, I feel quite honoured! ellen x'

I felt—on behalf of our little boat and the Trust—even more honoured. In fact I could hardly bring myself to believe it. To be quite sure, I made a point of tracking Ellen down at the Southampton Boat Show. By this time the promotional roller coaster was in full swing, and I had to use the Press Office events listing to work out on which stand she would be doing a photo call next. We managed to snatch a brief conversation. Yes, she did want to, really. A handshake and she was whisked away.

The next time we saw Ellen was after her triumph in the Vendee Globe. She came aboard *Nancy* the following summer during the Yarmouth, Isle of Wight, Old Gaffers Festival which she has been invited to open. She signed the Visitors Book ('Wonderful, dreamlike, and so very very real') as well as bits of paper, and the odd arm, proffered by the crowd of teenagers who had somehow materialized on the coachroof and foredeck (some of whom reputedly didn't wash the relevant part for a fortnight afterwards). Writing up the visit in her column for the *All at Sea* newspaper, Ellen described *Nancy* as 'a boat close to my heart, that of Arthur Ransome… She is in great shape still and sitting onboard her one can imagine him writing those famous books that must have inspired so many children (and maybe a few adults as well).'

On the water, however, the 2000 season was not going so well. In fact our visit to the Swamazons weekend (at which *Nancy* picked up the Concours d'Elegance award) was pretty much the high point of a frustrating season. It started late, the previous winter's repairs having caused *Nancy* to lose her place in the yard's work-schedule queue. Soon after launching, *Nancy* was involved in a minor collision. Not that serious in itself, but it helped bring to a head some of our organisational shortcomings. Managing *Nancy* involved a pretty steep learning curve, and one with a few sharp spikes. Our reporting procedures needed upgrading, and our operations manual came in for some criticism from a couple of skippers—new to *Nancy* but with experience in the sail-training world. At one stage we decided to suspend sailing entirely while we got to grips with these issues.

Once again the year ended with the death of a much-valued friend. Martin Lewis, a staunch supporter of *Nancy* and another person for whom the epithet 'enthusiast' seemed to have been invented, died at a ballet performance—another of his passions—of a massive heart attack, just a few weeks before the scheduled bypass operation which would have prevented it. Martin had been a Ransome fan since boyhood—an incorrigibly enthusiastic one, naturally. It was at his funeral, where many stories about Martin were exchanged, that I heard the story about Ransome calling at his boyhood house in Ipswich to give Martin a copy of his latest book with a request to to stop writing his long, detailed letters about boats and sailing. It surprised none of us. Martin was passionate, in a very thorough way, about all his enthusiasms, which included Shakespeare, the Labour Party and jazz as well as ballet and Ransome.

He lived near Pin Mill—his house, Sideways Cottage, was conveniently near the top of the drive leading to Woolverstone Marina—and sailed his Yachting Monthly Senior, *Pau Amma* on and around the Orwell. and he knew the area intimately. He could pinpoint *Goblin*'s mooring at Pin Mill, just a little upstream from the Hard, and he has mapped Secret Water. His support for *Nancy* and the Trust was unstinting—he was one of the first members of the initial appeals committee—and his faith in the project was simple and practical. He was one of those who felt that it had to succeed, and never doubted that it could. His cheerful grin, and his almost tangible enthusiasm and enjoyment were immensely sustaining.

Martin's death, coming so soon after Brigit's, caused me to reflect, not for the first time, on the true nature and value of preserving artefacts such as *Nancy*. People inevitably die; there's nothing we can do about it, they're made that way, disposable, recyclable. But they very rarely leave this earth exactly as they found it, and for some their influence is profound and enduring. That's certainly true of great writers, such as Ransome, and it is their possessions, the things they loved and touched, the houses they lived in, that help to bring to life their words, and to keep alive (at first as a memory, later simply as an awareness) some sort of contact with the person who wrote the words.

And how very much more true is this when the thing is question is something he wrote about, and how doubly true when that thing happens to be a boat, almost a living being itself, which he lived in, sailed, understood, interacted with, and probably at one time or another touched every inch of. And of course Ransome did not merely write about *Nancy*, or use her as a convenient prop in his story. He celebrated her, gave her a leading and active role in the tale, and through her poured out all that he loved, valued, even venerated about the act and the art and the deep, satisfying mystery of sailing the sea. That's why *We Didn't Mean to Go to Sea* is such a powerful book, and why *Nancy Blackett* is such a significant boat.

Martin understood this very well; it's apparent in a piece he wrote for *Mixed Moss*, the TARS journal, about the 'Great Race' with *Peter Duck* in 1994. It is one of the best ever descriptions of sailing *Nancy*, and I'm delighted to include in this book.

Two bright spots from 2000. At the Ipswich Festival that year, the last in the series, Alex Haig, who runs Anglia Yacht Brokerage, gave us two small black-and-white photos taken by his father. They show Arthur Ransome scrubbing *Nancy*'s bottom as she leans against the wall at Waldringfield, on the Deben, at low tide. The Haigs, who lived at Waldringfield, and the Ransomes appear to have been great friends—there's another photo showing a celebratory meal at Broke Farm, with Arthur, Evgenia and four members of the Haig family all wearing pirate hats. The Waldringfield photos probably relate to a trip in August 1937 when a loose nut on the propeller shaft necessitated *Nancy* being put against the hard there, and the problem inspected at low water. The result included these two very charming photos which also showed *Nancy*'s underwater sections off to advantage.

And then there were *Wizard*'s oars. *Wizard*, as *Secret Water* readers will remember, is the name Ransome gave to the dinghy used by the Swallows, but he borrowed the name from one of the trio of dinghies sailed by the children of his friend Major Busk, owner of *Lapwing*. The Eels in *SW* ('Pudding faces' to begin with, according to Roger) were based loosely on the Busk children, John, Jill and Michael, and *Lapwing* was of course the 'missionary ship'. *Wizard* herself sadly was no more; Major Busk had given her to a Scout troop, which had allowed her to rot away, but her oars were still with us, owned by Michael's widow Bridget, who lived near Andover and was keen to give them away to a good home. They are surprisingly long, at eight feet, and the blades, six inches wide, are tipped with copper. At present they clutter up my study. One day, perhaps, they might find, along with the cabin carpet, a permanent display.

We used this illustration ('Tied up in harbour') as a reference for rerigging *Nancy*

One advantage of a short and fairly inactive season was that very little winter work was needed, and *Nancy* could be back in the water good and early in 2001, ready for her seventieth birthday celebrations. And her birthday, according to her Certificate of Registry, was 30 March 1931.

No doubt her actual launch had been a bit earlier than that, but this was the only date we had to go on, and it was early enough for us. We decided to bring the AGM forward, to 31 March, which was the Saturday, and hold it for a change at Pin Mill Sailing Club. The club is a fair bit younger than *Nancy*—its founding more or less coincided with Ransome's departure from the area, and certainly post-dated the publication of *We Didn't Mean to Go to Sea*, so the oft-jumped-to assumption that *Goblin*'s masthead burgee is actually that of the Pin Mill Sailing Club is sadly erroneous (more probably the Royal Cruising Club, of which AR was a member). Still, it's a comfortable, welcoming sort of a place, a single-storey clubhouse towards the upriver end of the village, with a veranda and a splendid view out over the Orwell and, on this occasion, of *Nancy*, picking up a mooring offshore.

We always try to dig out some special treat or surprise for the AGMs and this time it was the black-and-white home movie footage of *Nancy* sailing under her previous owner—previous to Ransome, that is—the young Paget Bowyer, when she was still called *Electron*. The tape itself reached us in somewhat mysterious circumstances, being apparently an uncollected order from a video copying firm that was closing down, and which had somehow fallen into the hands of someone who recognised *Nancy* and assumed we'd be interested. Which of course we were. There was footage of her sailing in Poole Harbour (and of an ancient car boarding the chain ferry at Sandbanks) and of a cruise to the West Country—we can certainly identify Dartmouth, and probably Fowey. We can also clearly see that she had laid wooden decks (can't tell if it's teak) at the time. Interestingly, the final images on the reel show what must have been the Bowyer family's next boat, after they'd sold *Nancy* to Ransome. Its similarity, in size and shape, to *Selina King* is remarkable.

In the evening we held a dinner at the Butt and Oyster, in a deliberate nod to Mike Rines' relaunch dinner in 1989. A good few of the same people were there, including Mike himself of course, who brought a message from *Nancy* ('...I would like to thank Mr Ransome for giving me a respectable name...'), Christina Hardyment, Roger Wardale and Brian Hammett, as well as over fifty other members. The big dining room of the Butt was packed, with late-bookers being squeezed onto the ends of the horseshoe table, and there were toasts, a reading from *We Didn't Mean to Go to Sea* by the fine-voiced actor Gabriel Woolf who has recorded the entire series as audio books and who later became president of TARS. There were also musicians, shanty singing and cake. Fittingly, some of us stayed that night in Alma Cottage.

The early start to the season seemed auspicious for another Solent cruise, particularly as the second International Festival of the Sea (IFOS to its friends) was due to take place at Portsmouth again, at the end of August. It also enabled us to call in at Yarmouth Old Gaffers Festival and—as mentioned above—meet up with Ellen MacArthur. We also took *Nancy* to her first TARS AGM, which was being held that year at Southampton University. *Nancy* moored up at Buckler's Hard, a favourite destination of the Ransomes when they owned the two *Lottie Blossom*s, and the TARS—including president Norman Willis—came out by coach to visit her.

Then *Nancy* once again headed westwards, with the hope of making Falmouth, but this time contrary winds prevented her getting any further than Plymouth. They did however blow her back up channel in record time, skippered by Naval officer Jon Millward with his 12-year-old son Elliott forming part of the crew.

Thus it was that once again I found myself traversing Portsmouth Harbour, this time from the services marina at Haslar, and at a prudently early hour of the morning. It had been made clear to us that there was no provision in the arrangements to reserve pontoon berths for small boats which were likely to attract high numbers of visitors. It was first come, first served, so we were determined to be among the first. In this we were successful, and were allocated a perfect pontoon position beneath the broad apron which crosses the seaward end of Basin 2, and close by the foot of the ramp which led down to the pontoon. What we hadn't reckoned with however, was the profusion of people with 'bad legs' who had requested pontoon positions for their boats. I'd been away from the site most of the day, but the crew-member I'd left in charge had spent much of it fending-off requests from the berthing marshal to move *Nancy* to accommodate them—his excuse being that he wasn't 'authorized' to do so. Late in the afternoon, when I returned, the marshal renewed, more insistently, his demands that *Nancy* be moved—to the outer end of a substantial raft of boats. We argued our case, but were rapidly losing ground when who should come down the ramp but our book-stall manager, schoolteacher Jenny Wedick, in a wheelchair, with one leg plastered up and stuck out on a board. Most fortuitously, she'd ruptured her achilles tendon a week or two previously. Game over. *Nancy* stayed.

This was easily the most memorable and eventful IFOS of the three *Nancy* has now attended. Jonathan Cape, Ransome's publisher, now part of Random House, was about to relaunch the twelve books in a new paperback series, with dramatic, modern covers. Not to everyone's taste—the *Goblin* on the cover of *We Didn't Mean to Go to Sea* was a lurid pinky-purple colour—but they were intended to appeal to 'modern young readers' and attract attention on bookshop displays, both of which they did admirably. The launch date had been planned for September, but they decided to bring it forward so that it could take place on our stand, during the festival.

I was asked if I would go and be interviewed, about this and *Nancy* generally, over the Festival's tannoy broadcasting system. Only too glad to of course, and the more so when I discovered that this involved going up the Semaphore Tower, the hexagonal structure from which, before Morse Code and telephones, visual signals were sent, using a system of boards and shutters, by relay to the Admiralty in London, taking, it's said, under 15 minutes (and, so I've always assumed, the original of Terry Pratchett's clacks machines in his Discworld books). It's the tallest building in the dockyard, and normally closed to the public. Just now, appropriately enough, it was serving as the IFOS communications centre. This became a daily duty, and a delight, permitting me to enjoy the panoramic view across the harbour and the Dockyard, and, as I waited for my turn to go 'on air' to chat with some of the other people coming and going in the busy room. On one occasion, I found I was talking to someone who introduced herself as the ex-wife of the man who had done the cover illustrations for the Puffin editions of Ransome's books. Since Ransome's own illustrations were used for the original covers, and she was clearly neither Ivy nor Evgenia, I assumed she must mean Anthony Kerins, whose 1980s covers, lively and charming, are collectable in themselves.

Nancy's position across the end of the basin, prominent and a short step from the end of the ramp leading down to the pontoon, ensured once again a constant stream of visitors. It was also on the route for VIPs arriving by boat. Princess Anne passed by one day, pausing in her stride when she noticed *Nancy* and casting what we chose to interpret as a wistful glance at her, along with a few friendly words, before being bustled on by her minders.

By far my favourite meeting though resulted from an atmospheric chance encounter that same evening. It was about eight o'clock, quite dark, and quiet after the day-visitors had mostly gone home. I was returning to the boat when I came up behind two women, evidently a mother and daughter, at the top of the ramp, just in time to overhear the elder of the two almost whisper to her companion, 'Oh look, there's the *Nancy Blackett*,' Her voice was soft, but she spoke the words with a thrill of real excitement.

'Would you like to come down and have a look at her?' I interjected. Of course they would, and the younger of the two went off to fetch Dad, and a bottle of wine. It turned out they owned a Fairey Fisherman at the top of the basin, and were the Crossleys, Ian and Rosamund and daughter Julia. Soon all of us, them, me and *Nancy*'s other resident crewmember Roger Taylor, were all crowded into the cockpit enjoying the wine and chatting away as if we'd known each other all our lives.

Later, Princess Anne passed by again on her way back. Again, she paused—we lifted our glasses in what we hoped was both a respectful and a comradely manner—and she moved on to her waiting launch. One of her WREN minders paused for a chat on the way back, and revealed that she was a cousin of Francis Wheen, left-wing journalist and co-owner of *Peter Duck*.

Ian and Julia proved to be very well-qualified sailors and were instrumental in helping get *Nancy* home again at the end of the season.

Nancy hosted, and was helped by, many friends at that IFOS—Arwen Seccombe from Australia (her father is a big *The Lord of the Rings* fan) who seemed to spend much of the summer aboard her—she had also helped sail her down to Plymouth; Hilary Weston, who reached Portsmouth by means of a 100-mile sponsored cycle-ride from her home in Abingdon, and Jim and Judy Andrews from Windermere, who, no sooner than they has arrived were roped in to 'mind the boat' while I went off on some errand or other. Jim told me later it was 'a thrill and an honour' and how they'd enjoyed 'entertaining a young family and watching their emotions'.

Nancy's finest souvenir from the festival was a shanty that might have been (though in fact hadn't been) composed in her honour. That too was the result of a chance encounter. There was a little shanty-stage near the top of the ramp, and one day we got talking to a couple of singers, Alan Hardy and Ken Hunnybun who together performed as *Bitter End*. They revealed they had a song in their repertoire, called *Secret Water*, with the refrain 'Arthur's boat goes sailing on, all bound for Secret Water.' They came down onto the pontoon and serenaded *Nancy* with it. Its composer, Bob Watson, later told us that he'd written it as a tribute to Arthur Ransome, with the 'Arthur's boat' used as a metaphor. He hasn't known of *Nancy* or her history when he wrote the song, but its words, and its slow, lilting tune, fit *Nancy*, and her present role, like a glove.

The return from Portsmouth, with our new friends, Ian Crossley, a merchant navy captain as well as a seasoned yachtsman, and his capable 17-year-old daughter Julia, began well, with a spanking breeze for the up-Channel sail, but when about to enter Ramsgate Harbour the engine started playing up and *Nancy* had to be towed in by the lifeboat. Once the alternator was fixed, she set off again for home, but another failure—different problem—meant another call to the lifeboat. This time it was the Harwich boat that responded, but ironically distances and tides meant that the tow had to be back to Ramsgate.

At the end of the 2001 season, not surprisingly, we decided that the engine, which had been playing up all season, deserved a thorough overhaul, and arranged to have it lifted out. This revealed a number of cracked ribs. What appeared to have happened was that they had been previously cracked, and 'sistered' by way of repair—this is where an identical piece of timber is fitted, butted-up against the original to strengthen it. It's a well-attested practice, but in this case, only short lengths of new timber had been used, which in effect simply transfers the strain on the original timber to where the insert ends. Five ribs were affected, and it was described as 'long-term damage, certainly not recent', which made it odd that it wasn't noticed when the engine came out in 1999. The engine bearers were 'not a pretty sight' having evidently been made-do and mended, or adapted, over a number of engine installations, and were undoubtedly contributing to a high level of vibration.

Nancy was now — on the recommendation of Bill Wallace King, now boat manager — being overwintered at Woodbridge. This was much closer to her summer quarter on the Orwell than Southwold, which made for a shorter sea-voyage than Southwold at either end of the season, as well as being infinitely more convenient for most members. We had her laid-up at Robertsons boatyard there, and one thing that manager Mike Illingworth had quickly noticed was that the head of the mast, above the crosstrees, was unsupported, other than by the forestay, and this appeared to be contributing to the swan-neck curvature of that part of the mast. He wondered whether this had always been the case, and decided to check against Ransome's own illustrations in *We Didn't Mean to Go to Sea*. Not entirely to his surprise — though it's a tribute to the accuracy of Ransome's drawings — he discovered that there had indeed been a second pair of running backstays, leading from the top of the mast. (They are particularly clear in Ransome's drawing 'Tied up in Harbour', and also discernible in 'All but OB', 'Rescue at Sea' and 'Meeting the Sailing Ship'.) He immediately reinstated them and the mast has since become noticeably straighter.

Despite the engine problems — or possibly in part because they had happened and we'd coped with them — we ended the year in much better spirits than in 2000. *Nancy* had celebrated her significant seventieth birthday; she had successfully undertaken a long and difficult passage which had enabled her to be sailed by some fifty members under fifteen different skippers. She had been seen and visited by upwards of a thousand people, and a segment for a regional TV series hosted by Paul Heiney meant she'd been seen on screen by millions more. Our decision to move her winter maintenance to Woodbridge — made not without some heartache, as Harbour Marine at Southwold had served her, and us, very well over the years — felt like the right thing to do. At last we felt ready to tackle the one essential voyage that everyone had been waiting for *Nancy* to undertake ever since we acquired her.

CHAPTER FOURTEEN

Holland At Last

❧

One of Arthur Ransome's neatest tricks in *We Didn't Mean to Go to Sea* is his management of the sense of scale, as far as the crossing of the North Sea is concerned. The distance is only about 100 miles, and it takes around twenty-four hours in a boat of the *Goblin*'s size. For many yachtsmen it's a routine passage at the start or end to a summer cruise. English skippers regularly sail across to enjoy the Dutch inland waters, and Dutch yachtsmen, often in fleets of classic boats, come to the Orwell or the Deben, complete with tobacco-pipes and concertinas.

But for the four children aboard the *Goblin*, who have never previously sailed anything larger than a dinghy, anywhere larger than a lake, the North Sea is unimaginably large, and threatening. It poses new challenges in terms of tides and navigation, to say nothing of the wild weather. John has learnt how to read a chart, but they are soon off the edge of the only chart they've got. They are quite literally heading into the unknown. They have only the haziest idea of where they will land up on the other side.

Of course, as *Nancy*'s guardians we had to replicate the voyage of the *Goblin*, and Ransome's own 1936 voyage, aboard *Nancy* herself, and in 2002 we were ready to go. The script for this voyage, however, seemed perversely determined to be as different as possible from that of the *Goblin*. There were no children aboard, and two skippers rather than none (in fact three by the end of the crossing); the weather, apart from a token wisp of mist, was bright and calm, to the extent that the engine, which had plenty of fuel, was used for most of the crossing. Even the Beach End Buoy had turned from red to green (changes in the buoyage of Harwich Harbour having taken place since the 1930s). And Flushing was now Vlissingen—well, it always had been to the Dutch but in common with many another foreign location, it had shed the anglicized version of its name.

There was, as it happened, a Susan, girlfriend of skipper Pete Randall. The rest of the crew consisted of Bryan Bonser, rated skipper but acting mate for this leg of the trip, and Kat Bowmaker, one of Pete's professional yachting chums, whom he passed out as skipper at the end of their trip. And two Sinbads, stowed away at the beginning of the voyage for the purpose of staging the rescue partway across—both were cuddly toys, no actual kittens were dampened in these reconstructions.

Vlissingen proved to be full, so after a disappointingly uneventful voyage, *Nancy*, having entered the harbour without the assistance of a pilot, unlike the *Goblin* but like Ransome sixty-six years previously, motored on up the canal to Middelburg. As historic reenacts go, it was low-key, but even so the crossing rated a couple of column inches in *The Times*. And a reporter from the local Dutch paper, *PZC*, paid *Nancy* a visit (arriving a little late, as she'd originally been told to look for a boat called the *Goblin*) and wrote a long, and as far as we can tell accurate, piece which appeared as the main story on the front of the paper's weekend section.

And of course, we were never more than a few people away from a direct Ransome connection. The relief crew, Jenny Wedick and Sue Milward, coming up on the train to Goes, met an Englishwoman on her way to join her husband on their boat, who told them that the same husband, as a boy, was on a train in the Lake District, reading a Ransome book, when the large man in the opposite seat, none other than Ransome himself, leaned over and offered to sign it for him.

After a few days exploring the delights of the Oosterschelde and the Veersemeer, *Nancy* returned in some triumph to Vlissingen, welcomed by people on towpaths waving their copies of *PZC*, and the crew set out to reconnoitre literary locations. The windmill, spotted by the crew of the *Goblin* as they came in, was still there, though shrouded in scaffolding, and so of course was the lock, and still filled with jellyfish. Elsewhere, though, ex-Flushing appeared to have gone through some changes. Repeated attempts failed to locate the Post Office, and Kanaal Street was not where it should have been, or at least the street in question was called something else.

Mercifully, the old Fishing Harbour, where Cdr Walker had taken the *Goblin*'s crew for a meal, and where John's head, like Jim's, had drooped onto the tablecloth, was easy to locate, albeit now a marina, but the café they might have used was more of a problem—there were 10 to choose from.

Nancy's return voyage, though we'd dubbed it 'Commander Walker's passage', was more like Arthur Ransome's own return trip than the *Goblin*'s reverse-bearing dash back to Pin Mill and Mother. A long, four-day dogleg via Zeebrugge, Dunkerque and Ramsgate, back to Woolverstone and supper in the Marina restaurant, with skipper's and crew's heads all dipping Jim- and John-like towards their plates. The log records 'End of a historic and great voyage!'

As the *Goblin* leaves the lock on her way out of Flushing, Daddy remarks, 'We'll come across again some other time.' Who knows, perhaps they did. Perhaps John, 'years and years hence' when he was grown up and had a ship of his own, would have sailed her across to Holland and, as he had anticipated, remembered the night 'when for the first time ship and crew were in his charge and his alone'. But *Nancy*, and we, having done it once, were impatient to return the following year. We were also keen to at least partly replicate the *Goblin*'s trip by including actual children in the crew.

Now, families and friends hop aboard their boats and head off on long passages all the time without having to give any thought as to whether the make-up of the crew meet any external criteria. Not so, if you are an organisation such as the Trust. There are child protection requirements to be complied with as well as all the usual safety considerations, and it can be quite complicated making up a crew, particularly a small one, that meets all these regulations.

In the end, the crew comprised Bill Wallace-King, skipper and originator of the plan, his daughter Sabina (Beanie), aged 14, her friend Susie, 15, and another of *Nancy*'s accredited skippers, Ken Randall, shipping as Mate. (Another of our requirements, self-imposed in this case, is to have two skipper-grade crew on overseas passages.)

Although we had a Susan on board once more, who lived up to her namesake's reputation for being practical, capable and a good cook, the assignment of roles was a bit jumbled. Bill, as skipper was a lot more Rogerish than John-like, while Ken showed a very John-like streak, coming up with a comprehensive passage plan to save too much navigation work under way (not that John did, of course, things being the way they were, but you can bet he would have wanted to). And

although Susie was the practical one, it was Beanie, the dreamer, who showed a
thoroughly Titty-like attention to the shopping, making sure all the appropriate
foodstuffs, including the essential pork pie, were obtained.

Authenticity, as far as possible, was the aim of this crew. No gale-force westerlies, but they did survive a tremendous thunderstorm. Bill, like John, and indeed
Ransome, took the brunt of the helming through the night. The girls were wok-
en for their watch at 03.00, and noted in their log 'Being on watch really felt as
though we were part of the Walker children's adventure, fighting sleep, and in the
end we both couldn't help ourselves but to nod off in the cockpit for the second
half of our watch! Bill however was awake as he had been all day and steered for
us.' At the end of their watch, they handed over to Ken and were asleep as soon
as they tumbled into their bunks, but awake again by 09.00 to see Holland come
into view.

The engine was cut, and the reefs shaken out to start a wonderful sail up to
Flushing (as they preferred to call it). The Dutch courtesy flag was hoisted, and
below it, what Bill likes to refer to as 'the cheerful flag of Zeeland' (and it is, blue,
white and gold). The windmill was there, now devoid of its scaffolding, and then
it was through the very lock that is illustrated in *We Didn't Mean to Go to Sea*, and
round to tie up at *Goblin*'s old mooring. Here they discovered another change
to Flushing/Vlissingen—the quay is now used by small ships, so there are vast
intervals between the mooring posts, and the houses, and the shops selling clogs,
have all gone, bombed in the war, and replaced by a rather dreary row of apart-
ments. But never mind—they'd done it. For all of the crew it was the longest passage they'd done, and the farthest offshore, as it had been for the Swallows, and
for Ransome himself. Telegrams have been a thing of the past for a long while,
but texting now makes a very good substitute, so that was how the time-honoured
message was sent back, with multiple copies pinging off to various friends and re-
lations: 'Walker alma cottage pinmill goblin and crew increased by kitten all well
returning tomorrow night.' This prompted several replies, including a text-speak
version of Daddy's gruff compliment to John: 'ul b a c man yet'.

The text-telegram was however inaccurate in every respect, except 'all well'.
The crew had no intention of returning tomorrow night. Having reached Holland, they were determined to make the most of it, and join up with other boats

from the Old Gaffers Association to take part in the Dutch classic boat rally ending at Hellevoetsluis, which takes in Holland's own answer to Secret Water, and
much food, music and fun—as well as sailing and informal racing, in which Susie
proved their most focused helm. Here's an extract from their log:

Through the lock, a turn to starboard took us into the Steenbergsche Vliet, and off
all the Dutch charts. We have been sworn not to divulge the location of this marvellous place, so you may find the details very sketchy.

We sailed up a long canal/river, very similar to the Norfolk Broads, to Steenbergen, while Susie braided Sabina's hair using whipping twine for the ends. We
arrived to a great atmosphere with a big crowd and loud music. As we secured our
ropes a jolly man came aboard to welcome us with a red burgee depicting the old
harbourmaster's moustache, and gave us vouchers for raw herring and Corenwyn.
This was the feeder gathering for the Dutch Classic Yacht Regatta.

The girls started work in earnest, polishing the brass, and whipping the ends of
the warps, foresail sheets and fender ropes. Meanwhile, more and more of the most
beautiful classic boats we'd ever seen came in until the harbour was completely full,
and there was a big party in the evening with a Dutch band and dancing until way
after midnight. We really wanted to cross the harbour from one side to the other by
walking across the rafted boats, which spanned the whole harbour. The girls were
stopped, by a very merry Dutch lady, but Bill made it across later! The Dutch know
how to enjoy themselves and the party had a really relaxed atmosphere.

Wednesday—as Ken said on waking, 'How boring, another nice day'. SW
1/2, hot and sunny. One of the best parts of the trip was leaving Steenbergen, in a
long procession of beautiful yachts. In the lock, the girls got out their penny whis-
tles and played through their repertoire, to applause from the other boats and the
watching crowd. 'Keel Row' was the audience's favourite.

Once out of the Steenbergsche Vliet, it was a slow downwind sail in company
up the Volkerak. Everyone had all their sails up, which looked amazing. A stunning
mix of cream, white and tan with shiny varnish.

Because we had to have an early start next day we decided to avoid joining the
fleet in the old harbour at Willemstad and instead, headed for Numansdorp, a couple of miles across the Hollands Diep.

We found the entrance and crept in. The echo sounder lost its grip on reality at 0.9m but, having seen a boat come out, we bravely continued slowly up a delightful river, hoping the water would be deep enough. We reached the harbour, and were directed to 'box 19'. A Dutch 'box' involves motoring in between two posts to which stern lines are rigged, and lying bows to a wall or pontoon. Because of *Nancy*'s bowsprit, it was necessary to reverse in. The posts were intimidatingly close together, which turned out to be a blessing as the crew could walk the boat down between them on both sides at once. *Nancy* behaved beautifully, and after 14nM we were tied up at 19.00hrs and off up the long walkway to the town.

We selected the obvious restaurant at the head of the harbour, 't Schipperhaus. What a good choice. The ice creams were nothing short of magnificent. Early to bed for the crew, and a stroll down the walkway for Bill, who got within fifteen feet of a heron, and closer still to a probable badger in the undergrowth that he could hear but not see.

Then, for this crew—after an early-morning sail and a last hug for *Nancy*'s mast from Beanie—it was home on the ferry. For the next crew, however, things didn't go so well. *Nancy* developed engine trouble, and had to be left in a Dutch boatyard while it was fixed. Once it was, a rescue crew went out to bring her home.

After two years of 'going foreign'—and with some costly ferry trips to be got over—we decided *Nancy* deserved a quiet year at home in 2004, pottering about her local waters and giving some of the less-experienced sailors a chance to get to know her.

It also provided a chance for us to do something else we'd long wanted to, and that was to invite a group of schoolchildren aboard. It happened that the Year Nines at Thetford Grammar School (Beanie Wallace-King's school, but a year below her) were studying *We Didn't Mean to Go to Sea*, and headmaster John Woodgate was delighted at the offer to take some of them for a sail on *Nancy*. We sorted out a programme, with two groups, alternating between sailing and walking along the riverside path from Woolverstone to have a look at Pin Mill.

It was a beautiful day, and the voyage went well to begin with, but just about opposite Pin Mill, the engine started 'jumping about all over the place' according to those on board. It was quickly shut down, and the Woolverstone launch called up to assist us back to the marina. The problem proved to be that two of the four cast-iron mountings which attached the engine to the boat had fractured, one apparently some time previously, the other—which has been bearing the additional strain—there and then. The root of the problem seems to have been excessive vibration, caused by slight misalignment of the engine. Certainly, once it was fixed the engine seemed a lot quieter. As for the Thetford pupils, those on board probably enjoyed it more than a routine trip—and we found an alternative date for them later in the season.

Improvements to *Nancy* seem to come under two headings—distress purchases, like the various engine repairs, and the rest. Much of 'the rest' can be classed as planned maintenance, but some of it comes under the heading of 'pleasant surprises'. One such resulted from a chance observation by Jim Andrews at the previous year's TARS AGM, held at the Royal Hospital School, Shotley. Jim remarked that he'd often thought the staysail was rather small. And when we came to look at it, and compare it with the illustrations in the book, well, yes, it did look a bit as if it were trying desperately to be a storm staysail. The remark had coincided with an anonymous offer to fund a new one, and at the same time we received a donation in memory of an enthusiastic, and recently-deceased, supporter Mike Burton, which was enough to buy a new jib to match it. (The old jib was an embarrassment—it had been hastily repaired during one of *Nancy*'s south coast voyages with a fabric which though matched for colour was not of the right type, and showed up from miles off, or so it seemed to me, as a shiny strip right across the upper half of the sail.)

The new sails arrived in time for our 2004 AGM at the Royal Harwich, and the staysail was immediately bent on (the jib required a little more work before it could be used). The effect was immediately noticed by experienced *Nancy* sailors. The new sail, some fifty per cent bigger in area than the old one, was estimated to enable her to point five degrees higher and to add up to a knot, depending on the point of sailing, to her speed through the water.

We did find, though, that handling the new sail could be a bit of a challenge— *Nancy*'s sheeting arrangements are winch-free. Roger Sturge and I, sailing in an Old Gaffers event later in the season, evolved a sheeting routine for tacks which involved the staysail being caught and cleated as soon as it came over and then, if need be, working together to get the jib set as we wanted it and make any readjustments required to the staysail.

2005 brought another Portsmouth festival, but with a twist. This was the 200th anniversary of the Battle of Trafalgar, with a Fleet Review in its honour. *Nancy* was lucky enough to be selected as one of the flotilla of 400 small yachts invited to join a sail-past and salute the Queen. Less lucky was the sea-state on the day. Distinctly choppy, which made for an uncomfortable wait at anchor in the holding zone off Southsea Castle—though smaller yachts and those with short keels fared worse. Still there was plenty of interest to observe—150 warships of various nations at anchor, plus merchant vessels and fifty magnificent tall ships.

At about 1300 the red hull of Survey Ship HMS *Endurance*, bearing Her Majesty and the Royal party, emerged from the harbor and cruised past the moored ships before dropping her own anchor in preparation to receive the salute from our flotilla of yachts. At 1500 the call came over the VHF and we formed up into a loose phalanx of vessels approaching *Endurance* under engine, at a strict, and quite demanding, five knots.

Nancy found herself in line abreast with Sir Robin Knox-Johnston's world-girdling *Suhaili*, and as we turned into the run-up to *Endurance*, we were intrigued to see Robin himself on her foredeck, intently fiddling with some piece of equipment. This soon proved to be a small brass cannon, which—despite a standing instruction to the flotilla that there were to be no ordnance or pyrotechnics—he discharged with a satisfying bang and plenty of smoke just as our two vessels were making our turn to port under the sides of *Endurance*. We simply dipped our ensign, though not, I'll admit, the large pirate flag we were also flying. Sir Robin later told me he'd explained to the Queen's Harbour Master, who was in charge of the proceedings, that the Duke of Edinburgh would be 'very disappointed' if the cannon was not fired.

And so, the following morning, to our third, and sadly the last, International Festival of the Sea. A short, and early, hop over from Haslar Marina meant we would be in the forefront when the basins opened to boats at 7am. At exactly that time we reported to the Turning Marshall, based on a boat anchored in mid-harbour. 'What name?' he called.

'*Nancy Blackett*,' we replied.

'My heroine!' he beamed back, opening his arms in a gesture of welcome. Our plan paid off, and we secured a prime position on the central pontoon. Better still, for our stand, we'd booked a pitch alongside the main thoroughfare through the Festival, and right by the railings overlooking the basin. We could look directly down on *Nancy*, point her out to visitors and send them down to go aboard. We had a small caravan to brew tea and a gazebo to protect the stock, and were busy chatting to people from morning til night.

I often think these festivals were the best thing we did with *Nancy*. The sight of her stirs people's emotions, and they love to go aboard and sit in her cabin, just soaking up the atmosphere. We like to sail *Nancy*—we believe it's good for her to be used, and she makes a fine sight, and a great advertisement for herself on the river. It's also a tremendous experience for Ransome devotees who also happen to enjoy sailing. But for most fans, the act of sailing is something apart, which they just don't do—or for which their children are still too young—and just being aboard is a rich enough experience. It's fine for us, too. Being on static display means we can accommodate several hundred visitors on a busy day. And the Portsmouth festivals were the busiest. We've taken part in other festivals, at Ipswich, on the Thames in St Katharine Docks near Tower Bridge, and these days regularly at our 'second home port' in Woodbridge. All are enjoyable, but Portsmouth not only delivered greater numbers, it provided, more than anywhere else, that heady, exuberant feeling of being a part of a magnificent maritime tradition.

By 2006 it seemed about time to face the North Sea again. Not only was it the seventieth anniversary of Ransome's own voyage to Flushing, as research for *We Didn't Mean to Go to Sea*, it was *Nancy*'s seventy-fifth birthday, and also the tenth anniversary of the launching of the Nancy Blackett Appeal. It seemed right that as founder and chairman I should join the crew this time. We also determined that this passage would be a homage to Ransome himself and the passage he undertook, almost to the day, seventy years ago.

We set off from Woolverstone and picked up his route from Harwich, heading up to the Sunk and then setting a course of 105 degrees (or SE by E ½E in old money) straight on for Holland. Winds were light to negligible throughout ('between F3 and F-all'' according to the skipper). Modern yachts with engines can't resist the urge to turn them on when the wind, and their speed, falls below a

172 GOOD LITTLE SHIP

certain point, and neither could we. There is a practical necessity for this, too. In a Traffic Separation Scheme (a sort of dual carriageway for big ships), yachts are obliged to cross at right-angles, maintaining a minimum speed.

We were crossing one of these in early evening, at about a midway point in the voyage, when a shout went up from the cockpit of 'Dolphins!' I rushed up from the cabin, where I'd been chopping peppers for the evening meal, and there, indeed they were, three of them about 2 metres long, leaping and sporting around, diving under the boat. We slapped the sides of the boat to encourage them, and— in contravention of the TSS regs—slowed right down, though they seemed to prefer the noise of the engine at normal cruising speed. After about half an hour with us, they sped off like a pack of benign motorcyclists.

After the dolphins, and dinner, the wind got up sufficiently for us to hoist some sails and turn the engine off, meaning that each watch got a pleasant sail and a peaceful sleep below. It did drop our speed a bit, to 2.5 knots, but since we were aiming for an average of 3.5 knots and had some time in hand, we weren't unduly bothered. By about dawn though, the wind had dropped away so it was on with the little donkey again. In the end we made good time: ninety-nine miles in twenty-seven hours, compared with Ransome's ninety-three miles in twenty-five hours, but he measured from Shotley rather than upriver.

Once we reached Vlissingen we decided to deviate from Ransome's itinerary. Rather than continue past the windmill to the main dock, we moored up in the small marina (named after Michiel de Ruijter, the admiral who invaded the Medway in 1667) that now occupies the former fishing harbour. Like Ransome, but unlike the *Goblin*, we didn't bother to take on a pilot, though we were able to watch them buzzing busily in and out of their base next door. It's a convivial little marina, with its own café and close to the centre of town. We got talking to a yachtsman from a Dutch boat newly arrived from England who told us how, on their way over, his English crewmember had been telling them the story of the little boat that had drifted out of Harwich harbour with four children aboard who had managed to sail her all the way to Flushing... and had then been amazed to find her sitting there when he arrived.

To coincide with our visit, the local library had – with some help from crewmember and NBT trustee Bob Hull - put on a small exhibition about *We Didn't*

Mean to Go to Sea, and on our first day there we went to visit it and meet the librarian. We also, again, met up with a reporter from the local paper, the *PZC*, and in due course, again, we were front-page of the lifestyle section. One aim of this publicity-seeking was to see if we could find someone who would translate *We Didn't Mean to Go to Sea* into Dutch. This we eventually did, but not before we had resumed Ransome's route and motored up the Walcheren Canal to Middelburg, Veere and the Veersemeer. Veere is a delightful, well-preserved little town where Ransome's ne'er-do-well mate redeemed himself slightly and 'gallantly bought a tile for *Nancy*'. We attempted to do likewise, but failed—very few shops in Veere nowadays. We later found one in Middelburg, packaged up with some souvenir chocolates which I suppose was appropriate, and then another in a Vlissingen antique shop.

Our return to Vlissingen was, as on *Nancy*'s first voyage, greeted by towpath cyclists waving copies of *PZC*, Once back in the Michiel de Ruijterhaven, we were visited by a gentleman who volunteered to do a translation for us—which, within a few months, he did. *Swallows and Amzazons* and the other titles have been translated into various languages over the years—*S&A* even into Dutch, though long out of print—but it's always seemed something of an omission that *We Didn't Mean to Go to Sea* should not be available in Dutch (it's been translated into German, under the title *Die Unfreiwillige Seefahrt*). Unfortunately the translation wasn't as good as we'd hoped—some of the technical sailing terms defeated his skills and we are still, years later, trying to get them ironed out—and some people doubt the necessity of the whole exercise, given that so many Dutch people speak such excellent English, but we feel there is a certain symbolic rightness to the project, and still aim to complete it one day.

CHAPTER FIFTEEN

Twenty Years On

એન્જ

And all of a sudden twenty years have flown by. The germ that was sown in 1996 and grew into reality a year later continues, happily, to flourish. *Nancy Blackett* remains in rude health, and leads an active life, sailing on the East Coast and further afield, taking part in maritime festivals and generally feeding the flame of love for Ransome and his tales that seems to burn so brightly in so many sailors' souls.

For so many of our visitors, be they schoolchildren, nostalgic yachtsmen and women, or multi-generational family groups, *Nancy* is the *Goblin*, and it has always been our intention that she should live up to that identity. Authenticity has always been a primary aim, and we have tried to protect it in any decision we take affecting *Nancy*'s fabric, her appearance or her equipment. We want to hand on to future generations a boat that is recognisably Ransome's own, and the boat that the fictional Swallows, and Mother and Daddy, as well as all their readers, would have recognised as the *Goblin*. But also a boat that they can enjoy and appreciate by actually sailing her. This hasn't always proved easy or straightforward.

The classic example was the issue of guardrails, or lifelines—the 'fence' of stanchions and wires that runs around the edge of the deck on some boats. The idea is to stop people falling overboard. Many, but by no means all, modern yachts have them; there is a school of thought that, being about knee-high to an adult they can as easily contribute to accidents as prevent them. The *Goblin* didn't have them—they were far less common in those days—which is how John came to find himself 'almost O.B.' after reefing the mainsail. Almost, because he'd tied a length of rope, attached to the ship, around his waist, and that enabled him to scramble back on board. We use much the same principle, though the modern version involves jackstays—fabric straps running along the deck, to which personal safety lines can be clipped.

Less dramatic, but in a way more agonising, were the decisions regarding the cooker and the heads. Ransome did his cooking on a pressurised paraffin stove, almost certainly made by Taylors ('The stove in the galley burst into a roar'), and Mike Rines had installed an equivalent aboard *Nancy*. These stoves work well, when they work at all, but they do require skilled attention to get going, preheating the burners with methylated spirit, and needing particular care with the delicate mechanisms controlling the supply of pressurised fuel to the burners. They are a classic instance of a piece of machinery that responds well to the touch of its familiar owner. Which, with the variety of different skippers and crew, was exactly what *Nancy*'s stove didn't get. The result was frustration among cooks, and, all too often one or both burners out of action for weeks on end until expensive spares could be obtained and fitted. Sadly, the Taylors had to go. We replaced it with an Origo meths stove, which is not pressurised, and is simple to operate and thoroughly reliable, though lacking in personality.

As for the heads—the ship's toilet—it would seem there wasn't one on the *Goblin*, or at least its existence was discreetly passed over; that cutaway drawing isn't cut away enough to provide a view of it. In fact, or at any rate on *Nancy*, it's right in the forepeak, screened by a varnished wooden door, the invitation to open which always seems to delight and excite young visitors. The contraption itself was, when we acquired *Nancy*, a traditional 'Baby Blake' which looked as if it had been there forever, and probably had, complete with brass fittings and a wooden seat, which I always felt was the closest you could get to Ransome aboard the boat. Alas, though, its mechanisms were getting worn, and it—and hence *Nancy*'s bilges—were becoming distinctly unhygienic. It had to go, and was replaced by a modern appliance from a chandlery catalogue. With a plastic seat.

Replacing the engine ought to have been an easier decision, though surprisingly at the time there was some resistance to the idea among the board of trustees. It wasn't as if this was in any way original – far from it. *Nancy* had originally been fitted with a Thornycroft 'Handy Billy', a small, petrol-driven 'auxiliary' engine rated at nine bhp on *Nancy*'s Certificate of British Registry. Even though it was quoted on the certificate as being capable of six knots, about *Nancy*'s hull speed, this would have only been under the most benign conditions; 'auxiliary' meant just that, a helping hand when the assumption was that the wind provided the main motive power, and if it failed you dropped the anchor and waited. It wasn't compatible with the boating habits of time-poor modern yachtsmen who keep their boats in marinas. And in any case, it had long gone by the time Mike Rines found and restored *Nancy*—in fact there was no engine at all.

Mike's choice of a replacement had been a reconditioned three-cylinder diesel engine, Thornycroft-badged, although made by Mitsubishi. It was powerful, but huge and heavy, and very noisy. Conversation between cockpit and cabin, and on the VHF, was difficult, sometimes impossible. It also vibrated horribly. This caused it to break free from its mountings in 2004 and during its removal for their replacement, we discovered that it had apparently been responsible for cracking a number of the immediately adjacent ribs. Nevertheless, it was reinstalled, on dampened mountings, and staggered on until the end of the 2007 season, by which time we had raised sufficient funds to pay for a replacement.

The new engine, installed over the 2007/8 winter lay-up, was a Nanni 3.2-litre diesel, 21bhp, installed 2008, rated only 2bhp lower than the old Thornycroft, but significantly smaller, lighter, more powerful, and a great deal more fuel-efficient. And quieter—that first season with the Nanni was a joy and a revelation. It is probably—no, definitely—the most significant improvement to the experience of sailing on *Nancy* that we've made.

We've also introduced some discreetly-located up-to-date electronic navigational aids—as well as VHF radio, we now have GPS and AIS ship-spotting technology—all the things that would have saved the *Goblin* from having to make her unplanned voyage. And we have a range of informative instruments: speed and direction (the wind's and our own) as well as depth of water, displayed on a trio of wireless little TackTick screens that can be hidden away at a moments's notice to preserve the period ambience.

In fact, we've managed to avoid changing very much at all, certainly anything essential, even though *Nancy* is now eighty years older than when Ransome owned her, and we've owned her a lot longer than he did.

Ransome immortalised her in his two books, and then moved on—though he often regretted it. He regarded *Nancy Blackett* as 'The best little boat I ever had'. But maintaining something immortal can be quite a responsibility. It's a tribute to Mike Rines and his shipwrights—who I recently discovered included the late

Nancy Blackett at the Maritime Woodbridge festival

Readying for her relaunch after the winter refit

Mick Newman, co-founder of Spirit Yachts—that her restoration thirty years ago has enabled *Nancy* to survive as well as she has.

But time does take its toll—and insurers do require surveys at regular intervals. The most recent was at the end of the 2015 season. We have I think been very fortunate in our choice of surveyors over the years, but this time we felt a fresh pair of eyes would be a good idea. So our boat management team cast around using the usual criteria for selecting a surveyor, and came up with a name. When I asked the name of the chosen surveyor I was intrigued to find it was James Pratt, none other than the young boatbuilder whom Mike Rines had employed on *Nancy*'s restoration after his boat had broken loose and drifted up onto the Levington shore near Mike's house thirty years ago.

James has proved to be an excellent, thorough surveyor with a great nose for those hidden areas where trouble can lurk. As a result *Nancy* got quite a few new floors (important, hidden structural pieces that link the frames to the keel—the part of the cabin, or the cockpit, that you walk on is known as the sole), and several other things, plus a to-do list with quite a few less urgent things for the next winter lay-up.

In addition, the mast suffered two cracks in two years. The first, discovered at the end of the 2014/15 winter lay-up, was a major split near the crosstrees. We decided to cure it with a scarph, (inserting a new length of mast with a logitudinal diagonal glued joint), partlly because it was quicker to do than make a new mast, and the time for relaunch for the new season was almost upon us, but also it was the cheaper option and seemed—and probably was—adequate.

But then, at the end of the next winter lay-up, another crack was found—much smaller, an L-shaped hairline about 6in long, and much lower down the mast. James prescribed a temporary glassfibre and gauze bandage, accompanied by a recommendation to sail 'conservatively' (not above force four). At the end of the season, we had a good look at it, and discovered that over the years it had developed some strange deformities—and according to James, was actually thinner than it ought to be. We reckoned it was at least thirty years old, though probably not original. (Someone told me recently that Hillyards' masts were square-sectioned and hollow—like a box girder presumably – though I've no other evidence of this.)

Clearly the time had come to invest in a new one, which was made in early 2017 at Collars in Oxfordshire, with the fitting and new standing rigging carried out by Robertsons. Boatbuilders like to talk of giving a boat a 'birthday' when they give it a particularly thorough overhaul, so a new mast seemed a particularly appropriate birthday present for *Nancy*, even if the significant anniversary was the Trust's, rather than her own. With another trip to Holland planned for 2017, to mark the eightieth anniversary of *We Didn't Mean Go to Sea* being published, it was important to have *Nancy* in tip-top condition.

In fact 2017 turned out to be a triple anniversary—it also marked the fiftieth anniversary of Ransome's death, which qualified him to be include in an initiative by the tourist board Visit England, called '2017—Year of Literary Heroes'. This was eagerly taken up by a recently-formed 'Tourism Action Group' for the Shotley Peninsula, where Pin Mill is located, and led to a host of ideas and projects, including permanent innovations such as The Arthur Ransome Trail, running along the Orwell from the Butt and Oyster to the Bristol Arms at Shotley, and information boards at key locations. The Nancy Blackett Trust is a founder member of the group, and among our proudest contributions is the generic name for the area, 'Arthur Ransome's East Coast,' adopted by the Shotley Peninsula, but in effect also covering the other side of the Orwell, including Levington and Felixstowe, as well as 'Secret Water', The Walton Backwaters.

We also sponsored, with help from the Heritage Lottery Fund, an exhibition based on Ransome's own photos of the building of *Selina King*. The trip to Holland did take place, and lasted two months, with eight crews enjoying sailing on the Veersemeer and the Oosterschelde. It was preceded by a celebratory flotilla, organised by the Royal Harwich Yacht Club, down the River Orwell. And we rounded the season off with a marathon reading of *We Didn't Mean to Go to Sea* at Pin Mill.

Although supposedly tourism-oriented, many if not all of the initiatives seem to be equally and in some cases more for the benefit of the locals, with the aim of improving their awareness of the area they live in. This is particularly true of schools, where the Trust has assisted with a number of projects, and has been able to develop contacts with the local schools, something that had proved surprisingly difficult up to now.

As for myself, in 2013 I concluded that I had hogged the role as chairman of the board of trustees for long enough, and stood down in November. The members kindly organised a whip-round to buy a present for me; I chose a specially commissioned painting of *Nancy* by Claudia Myatt, and we had a party at the Royal Harwich. Roger Sturge took over as chair. At the AGM the following summer, they elected me as president, a post that had been either non-existent or vacant since the Trust's inception, despite the appointment of a number of honorary vice-presidents. The event was marked, appropriately I felt, by a cruise down the Orwell of Ransome's three locally-owned boats, *Nancy Blackett*, *Peter Duck* and *Ragged Robin III* (ex-*Lottie Blossom*), surprisingly, perhaps, the first time all three had been together on this river. The weather was dreary, but it brightened enough for us all to raft up opposite Levington and share some champagne. Julia Jones, *Peter Duck*'s owner, had been adamant that it was not to be a rerun of the Great Race, as I'd initially hoped for, and it wasn't. However, when we sailed back, under clearing skies and a decent breeze, *Peter Duck* started first but by the time we passed Pin Mill, *Nancy* had overhauled her. Just saying. Perhaps they were being kind.

Since then I've been trying to work out what a president does, or doesn't do. The answer, in my case, seems to be what I'd always wanted, to be a free spirit who doesn't have to get involved in the work of management and admin (and indeed ought not to unduly interfere in it) and who can spend his time on the sort of projects—like the Ransome anniversary—that breathe life, movement and development into the Trust.

I'm fond of saying people pass away, but boats, like books, can live forever. It's true, though it does require some qualification. Books do possess intrinsic qualities, though the value and recognition accorded to them will vary among succeeding generations. And a boat will only survive if it is cared for and maintained by someone, or ones, who care for it and know what they're doing. Even then, there's an inevitable deterioration which can be hard to spot, and increasingly costly to reverse. Judgment will have to be exercised, and funds raised. The conditions under which *Nancy* can be allowed to sail may need to become increasingly restrictive, to a point where she has to become a static exhibit—still, one hopes, an object of inspiration but no longer the living, breathing creature of the sea she was built to be.

Hopefully that day is far off; maybe it will never come. Meanwhile, however, *Nancy*'s cabin is still lit by oil lamps, which cast a mellow glow over the varnished mahogany, though they may not be all that conducive to in-bunk reading (head-torches are popular among more experienced crew members). It is still possible, if you're so minded, to imagine yourself one of the Swallows. Titty's bunk is still Titty's bunk, as are John's, Susan's and Roger's, and they are still blue. There is still a little brass handle for reefing, the brass porthole in the cockpit that still won't stay bright, and, if you move the GPS out of the way, a compass with a card marked with the cardinal points for steering in the old-fashioned way: 'south-east by east... south-east... south-east by south'.

In *Coot Club*, Mrs Barrable urges her reluctant pug-dog William to venture across the mud to establish a link between the two stranded boats with the words: 'Now William, this is your moment. It comes to everybody, just once, the moment when he has to be a hero, or not think much of himself for the rest of his life.' It's a nice joke, given that the exhortation is presumably lost on William, but one gets the sense that Ransome himself was no stranger to such situations. These challenges arise in various forms; they don't always call for a 'heroic' response, but they do change the lives of those who hear them and *Nancy* seems to have a habit of throwing them out. To Ransome she set him a new benchmark in both sailing and storytelling. You could say that *We Didn't Mean to Go to Sea*, and the experiences that led up to it, were a rite of passage for him, as well as his characters. To Mike Rines, she appealed as a pretty boat in need of restoration, and ended up demanding of him a great deal more than he'd been initially expecting. And in me she found someone who, much to his own surprise, could not turn away from the task of ensuring her continued preservation. If a boat can be said to have a soul, and of course no sensible person believes that for a minute, then *Nancy*'s is that of a survivor, and one which inspires the best in those who surround her. Or as John put it, 'So long as the *Goblin*'s all right, we're all right.'

Arthur Ransome's Pin Mill and Environs

❧

For Arthur Ransome, Pin Mill was 'this happy place where almost everybody wore sea-boots and land, in comparison with water, seemed hardly to matter at all.' Here is how he describes it at the beginning of *We Didn't Mean to Go to Sea*: 'Only the evening before they had come down the deep green lane that ended in the river itself, with its crowds of yachts, and its big brown-sailed barges, and steamers going up to Ipswich or down to the sea. Last night they had slept for the first time at Alma Cottage.' The Pin Mill Ransome knew is little-changed today. You can still see Alma Cottage, where the Swallows stayed, and the Butt and Oyster, where Jim Brading, skipper of the *Goblin*, was hoping to get 'breakfast' at 7pm, is still serving food and drink. The river still laps its walls at high tide, and then retreats, leaving 'boat after boat high, but… not exactly dry on the shining mud.'

Arthur Ransome and his wife Evgenia moved into the area in 1935, soon after he made his name as author of *Swallows and Amazons*, first published in 1930, and five of its successors. They knew East Anglia—he had already set one book, *Coot Club*, on the Norfolk Broads, and he had family connections with the long-established machinery firm of Ransomes in Ipswich. It's rumoured that their choice of the Shotley Peninsula was arrived at by Evgenia sticking a pin in a map. In the end, they rented a house, Broke Farm, now Broke House, at Levington, on the other side of the river Orwell and a mile and a half downstream. Subsequently, about 1938, they moved to Harkstead Hall, on the Pin Mill side of the river and about a mile inland.

There are three ways of reaching Pin Mill, if you include arriving by boat. One of the most pleasant is via the wooded, riverside footpath from Woolverstone Marina, about a mile away. But most people will arrive by car, dropping down that half-mile of 'deep green lane' from the B1456 Shotley road at Chelmondiston.

There's a small municipal carpark these days, on the left, just above the village. Assuming you've left your car there and continued by foot into the village, you'll soon come abreast of a black garage door on your right, and facing onto the lane. Above its lintel a small board proclaims 'Alma Cottage'.

The building is L-shaped, set back and above the lane on an embankment, but with the one wing stretching out to the road, with the garage underneath it. This wing is the present-day Alma Cottage, and you might think Miss Powell would have been hard-pushed to get six full-board lodgers and herself into it. In fact, the whole of the building you see, now divided up into three separate residences, used to be Alma Cottage, and in previous times it was the Alma Inn. There really was a Miss Powell, born there when the cottage was still the inn, and in Ransome's day she ran it as a tea-room and a guest-house. One thing she didn't originally have on the menu though was omelettes—but she quickly learned to make them once *We Didn't Mean to Go to Sea* was published.

There was also a Mr Powell, Annie Powell's brother John, 'Practical Sail Maker and Ship Chandler' whose loft was located in the lean-to at the end of the cottage nearest the river. We have a copy of an invoice made out to Mr Ransome and 'yacht *Nancy Bracket*'. He evidently took a fairly relaxed approach to business since it is dated 12 January 1938 (shortly after *Nancy* has been sold) but covers various items supplied between March and June 1937. He must have been at least the second, probably the third, generation, since the invoice's letterhead states: 'Established 1859'. The late John Leather recalled (in an article for *Classic Boat*, December 2004) visiting Pin Mill in 1950 and taking a torn sail up to Mr Powell for repair. He described 'a squat, irregular building' that 'stretched back up the hillside, backed by a copse of trees.' Inside the dimly lit sail loft, 'the floor, surprisingly, followed the slope of the hillside, its time-polished boards carried the chalked-out shape of a sail... at the far end of this artificial cavern, uphill, rotund John Powell, the sailmaker, sat bespectacled and comfortable on his bench.' More recently, with the floor levelled, the lean-to extension has been a shop and chandlery, run for many years by the harbour-master, Tony Ward. These days it is primarily a photographic gallery with a small trade in cards and ice-creams.

Below Alma Cottage, the lane does indeed do its best to end in the river itself. The formal road bears round to the right, but it is easy enough to drive—

or walk—straight on down onto what is Pin Mill's most distinctive feature, the Hard. This narrow, concreted causeway runs straight down into the river, coming to an end at about the half-flood mark. It's accompanied on its upstream side, by the Grindle, a modest tributary of the Orwell that gouges as it goes a useful channel which enables people rowing ashore from boats to haul their dinghies well up. Either side of the Hard is an area of light-coloured, firm mud (decreasingly so in both respects as you approach the river) where boats can be hauled up and grounded on a spring tide so that work can be done on them. There might be a barge or two moored off here, though far fewer than in previous years when their masts and sprits formed a permanent part of the Pin Mill skyline, captured in innumerable water-colours and photos.

One of the best places to contemplate this scene, along with the river traffic and the green wooded banks opposite, is the big bay window in the bar of the Butt and Oyster pub. Situated just below Alma Cottage, right on the high tide-line, or indeed a little below it, the 'Butt' has a long history, with the courts of the water-bailiffs and the burgesses of the Port of Ipswich held here as far back as 1542. The present building dates from the 17th Century and is Grade II listed. The pub has an inevitable association with smuggling. More recently the Ransomes might have stumbled across Edward VII and Mrs Wallace Simpson who apparently used the pub as a secret rendezvous while she was awaiting her decree nisi to come through at Felixtowe. The stone-flagged bar, with its fireplace, high-backed settles and good ale drawn straight from barrels behind the bar, is undoubtedly much as Ransome knew it, though the dining-room off it has been remodelled on two levels since Mike Rines held his celebratory dinner for *Nancy*'s relaunch in 1989, and the Nancy Blackett Trust held another in honour of *Nancy*'s seventieth birthday in 2001.

If you follow the lane from Chelmondiston, as it bears to the left, away from the Butt, you'll find yourself skirting the small bay on which Pin Mill is set, and in which there are many yacht moorings laid. *Goblin*'s was here, as would have been *Nancy*'s. To your left, inland, once you've passed the public conveniences, you'll find Webb's yard, a firm with a long history of barge building and repair. Then there's the Common. Immediately past the Common is another site of significance to Ransome pilgrims, the sprawling yard of Harry King & Sons. The yard dates back to around 1850, when it was started by William Garrard. It was taken over by his apprentice Harry King in 1898. The large wooden sign in front of the yard is over 100 years old—it was repainted when the yard became King's—but it used to hang on the main shed. King's built two boats for Arthur Ransome: *Selina King* in 1938, and *Peter Duck* in 1946. Ransome was good friends with the Kings, hence the adoption of their surname for his first boat (the *Selina* was a fancy of Evgenia's, though by coincidence also an aunt of Harry King's). Although it's now more concerned with restorations and repairs, the yard built over a thousand boats in its time.

Beyond King's you'll come to the Pin Mill Sailing Club, of which Ransome was a member. It is a hospitable place and the view of the Orwell from its verandah is splendid; visiting yachtsmen are welcome when the bar is open.

To the north-east there is a footpath along the river; start by going up the lane beside the sailing club. It runs to Woolverstone, about a mile away, providing beautiful views and easy walking, though there are a few places where it can be muddy. *Nancy Blackett*'s summer home is Woolverstone Marina. The Royal Harwich Yacht Club is also located here. On the downriver side of Pin Mill, there's another footpath, starting below the Butt and Oyster and leading past a few houseboats. This becomes slightly more challenging, narrow, and with foliage and brambles to contend with. It follows the river right round into the Stour to the Bristol Arms at Shotley, and is now known as the Arthur Ransome Trail.

Arthur Ransome would have rowed or sailed between his home at Levington and Pin Mill in his dinghy *Coch-y-bonddhu*. Or he might have driven round the head of navigation, through Ipswich, passing the dock. Nowadays, the road route across the river is via the Orwell Bridge. The drive from Pin Mill, back along the B1456, passes the head of the half-mile drive leading to Woolverstone Marina, and a lay-by with a good view of the river at Freston Reach. Just before the mini-roundabout for the slip road to the bridge is Fox's Marina, where *Nancy*'s 1988-89 restoration was carried out by Mike Rines. Even with the bridge, it's a surprisingly long way to Levington by road—around 10 miles from Pin Mill.

There are two main sites of Ransome interest in Levington. One is his house, Broke Farm as it then was, Broke House today. A comfortable old redbrick buiding, it faces the river and provided Ransome with a broad view of it, from Har-

Pin Mill, with the Butt and Oyster, and to the right part of Alma Cottage (as was)

NBT members visiting Ransome's former home, now Broke House

wich Harbour right up to Pin Mill and beyond, from the room upstairs which he chose to write in. Broke Farm was the home farm to the other building of interest, Broke Hall, about half a mile away. It was here that two children whom Ransome befriended, George and Josephine Russell, lived. They met him soon after they moved in, down at Levington Creek, where he was pulling in his dinghy. They crewed for him on *Nancy*, and he lent them *Coch-y-bonddhu*. Broke Hall, or to be precise a converted outbuilding in its grounds, was also the home of Mike Rines when he bought and restored *Nancy Blackett* in the 1980s. In 1999, *Coch-y-bond-dhu* rested in his yard for a few weeks between the Old Gaffers Secret Water race and the Ipswich Maritime Festival. Historically, Broke Hall is of interest as the home of the Broke family, of whom Captain Philip Broke RN won a distinguished victory in the American War of Independence. His HMS *Shannon* took on the more heavily armed USS *Chesapeake* outside Halifax, Nova Scotia, and defeated the notionally superior vessel in less than 15 minutes. A good description of the battle, lightly fictionalised, appears in Patrick O'Brian's *The Fortunes of War*, along with a passage describing Broke Hall and the river.

To further follow Ransome's wake it's best to take to the water. Supposing we join *Nancy Blackett* at Pin Mill, or more probably, for ease of access, Woolverstone, and drop down the river, with *We Didn't Mean to Go to Sea* on the cockpit seat, open at Chapter IV. One thing you'll quickly realise, as you tick off the green conical buoys on your port hand, and the red cans to starboard is that the buoyage system in the river has changed since Ransome's day. 'Red buoys and conical buoys to starboard. Black can buoys to port,' explains Jim Brading. 'That's coming up with the flood,' he adds. 'So we leave the conical ones to port now, because we're going out, not coming in.' He points to a conical one off Levington Creek, and another, just ahead, and a black can buoy to starboard off Collimer Point. This was, in effect the opposite of the British system in use at the time, which was red cans to port, black cones to starboard. Because of its trade connections with Holland, the port of Ipswich adopted the Dutch buoyage system, and continued to do so until about 1950, when it was brought into line with the rest of the UK. Things changed again in 1977 when the present IALA system, green cones to starboard, red cans to port, was introduced.

Keep an eye open on the port hand for a few landmarks on the north bank. A good view of Broke Hall opens up and, if you're quick, a glimpse of Ransome's old home at Broke House. Below Levington, there's Fagbury Point, where the *Goblin* saw the green boat aground. Then the river bears round to the left, you pass, officially, into Harwich Harbour, and the Felixstowe container terminal comes into view. This definitely wasn't there in Ransome's day, though Felixstowe was a port then. As you pass over Felixstowe's North Shelf, where the *Goblin* dropped her anchor on that fateful morning, you can still spot, below all the cranes and banks of containers, the little slip between the pier-heads where Jim rowed ashore for petrol.

On the other side of the river, you'll already have spotted Shotley Point, with its water tower, and what looks vaguely like the mast of a tall ship. It serves as a reminder of the naval base, HMS *Ganges*, that used to be here, and to which Commander Walker had been posted. Further down is Harwich, 'the little grey town with its church spire and lighthouse tower.' It's a picturesque, if sleepy little place, worth a short visit if you can find a space to tie up on Halfpenny Pier (free in the daytime, despite its name).

Between Shotley and Harwich lies the river Stour, where the *Goblin* went to drop anchor on the first evening. The pub where they went to buy grog and phone Mother is easily visible—It's called the Bristol Arms and is right by the Bristol Pier, which the crew of the *Goblin* used to walk ashore. Apart from this one visit, the Stour doesn't feature in the *Goblin*'s voyages, but it's worth exploring, peaceful compared to the busy, commercial Orwell. There's a fine view of the magnificent Royal Hospital School, with its clock tower, and on the opposite bank, Wrabness, with its little beach, is ideal for swimming, or a barbecue. Further up, you can reach the pleasant towns of Mistley and, with care, Manningtree. Back in Harwich harbour, continuing south beyond Landguard Point will bring you to the Beach End buoy, then a red parrot cage with a bell in it, now green with a solar panel attached. Go beyond it, and you will be out at sea.

If you do choose to venture beyond the Beach End buoy, you can potter north-east along the coast, past Felixstowe's seafront, and negotiate the shifting sandbar into the river Deben. This is a familiar route for *Nancy Blackett*, as she overwinters at Woodbridge, nine miles up the river. As you come into the river, you'll pass (or pick up a mooring and visit) the funky fishingboaty little hamlet of

Felixstowe Ferry (good pub and an excellent 'full English breakfast' café). Across the river the last remaining radar mast is a reminder of the 'tall wireless masts at Bawdsey' supposedly spotted by the *Goblin* on her return voyage. 'Supposedly' bcause although they had been erected by the time Ransome knew the area, from 1935 onwards, they weren't there in the year the book is set, 1931.

Woodbridge is a delightful town, well worth a visit, by boat up the delightful river, or by land (goodish train service, very convenient station), perhaps to visit *Nancy* in her winter quarters and help with preparing her for the next season. Ransome brought *Nancy* into the Deben on at least three occasions, twice in 1937 in August and October, and again in June 1938. He always made for Waldringfield, where he had an acquaintance. We have two photos of him scrubbing her off at Waldringfield, which somebody brought to *Nancy* when she was taking part in one of the Ipswich maritime festivals. He visited Woodbridge at least once, to give a talk at the Deben Yacht Club.

South-west from Harwich quickly brings you to the Walton Backwaters, the setting of *Secret Water*. They are less of a secret than they once were, though the entrance is still hard to spot until you get quite close—the trick is to find the Pye End buoy. The map drawn by the 'Secret Archipelago Expedition' in the book is still very recognisable, and fun can be had comparing the names with those on a modern chart. Swallow Island (in reality Horsey Island) is still there, though these days camping is not permitted, and nor is casual visiting, though an occasional organised trip, walking across the famous Wade, is arranged by the local region of the Arthur Ransome Society. The Wade, a causeway uncovered at low tide, is extremely muddy and rutted, and hard work, especially for small children. Many a wellington has had to be abandoned. The four posts midway along the Wade, which are a major feature of the book, are no longer there. Many locals doubt if they ever were. Not too far from the Wade at its 'mainland' end, Witches Quay (Kirby Quay) is still an attractive spot, with its thatched cottage. Another annual event, usually in mid-July, is the 'Round Swallow Island' dinghy race organised by the Old Gaffers Association; it starts from the Walton & Frinton Yacht Club in Walton-on-the Naze (the initials YC are just visible on the Swallows' map, in the blob dismissively marked 'Town'). This is one place where a dinghy can be launched—another is Titchmarsh Marina, which wasn't there in

Ransome's day. Though many more boats now seem to know the way into the Backwaters, the area still has a peaceful, remote feel about it. Drop an anchor in one of the less-frequented parts on a summer's evening with the cries of seabirds echoing against the sky, and the world of Ransome, and Maurice Griffiths, is instantly recreated.

Ransome's Other Boats

☙

Arthur Ransome owned more than a dozen boats in his lifetime. They varied enormously in size, type and duration of ownership. And, inevitably, in importance. The list that follows is an exercise in completism, logging all known boats, but it also gives considerably more space to some than to others. Where possible, it also describes what happened to the boats after they had left Ransome's ownership. The list divides, more or less, into four main periods, linked to four significant locations, but begins somewhat uncertainly with an unknown boat, of which the only evidence is a couple of sidelong references in letters to his mother in 1917-18.

On 26 February 1917, speculating on a more rosy future, he wrote—referring to his sister Joyce—'We will live on my boat. Said yacht is meanwhile decaying away, and will be in an awful state when the war is over. Still I daresay with plenty of candle grease in the worst leaks she'll float in still water and allow me to sit in the cabin and hammer out books worth writing.'

Towards the end of 1918 he wrote 'I shall bring my yacht round from Southampton… My boat must have some sort of harbour to lie in, she being too big and deep-keeled to be beached.' These were his Russian years, and it seems likely that the boat was an impulse purchase, made regardless of condition, which was clearly poor, to provide some sort of link with England. There's no record of what happened to her, and he was soon busying himself, and Evgenia, with real boats…

Slug was 'a long, shallow boat with a cut-off transom that had once carried an outboard motor,' according to Ransome, writing in his autobiography. He came across her while walking along the beach at Reval (now Tallinn), Estonia in 1920, where he found her being given a 'lick of green paint' by her owner. Beside her

Slug (1920), Reval, Estonia

Kittiwake (1921), Reval

were some large round boulders which proved to be her ballast. She was an open boat, about eighteen feet long, clinker-built, with very little depth of keel as far as one can tell from the only surviving photograph (included in the 2003 reissue of *Racundra's First Cruise*, edited by Brian Hammett). She had a short mast, a very short bowsprit, and a patched sail, which eventually got stolen. She was very slow, which is why Ransome and Evgenia called her *Slug*.

Kittiwake, the Ransomes' next boat, purchased in 1921, was smaller than *Slug*, at sixteen feet overall, six feet beam and five feet draught, but she had a little cabin, and a deep keel, along with a blunt nose and a long counter stern. Ransome, no doubt inspired by E. F. Knight's *Falcon on the Baltic*, had been planning to obtain and convert a ship's lifeboat, shipped out from England, but his 'agent' Captain Jackson of the SS *Cato* had been unable to buy one. They, he and Evgenia, began to think of building one instead, but settled for buying one off the beach at Reval so as not to lose a summer's sailing. She was a 'stout, dumpy little yacht,' carvel built in Finland. They called her *Kittiwake* after a picture of a gull in a bird book, and imagined they were the first to think of it. Later they were to discover 'flocks of Kittiwakes in English waters.' Ransome considered her 'a bit of a joke really'—but hardly as much as the dinghy he had built, by a firm of undertakers, to row out to her. It was triangular, and prone to capsize 'if I shifted my pipe from one side of my mouth to the other'. They sailed her throughout June and July, but evidently abandoned her when they moved to Riga, Lativia in 1921. They later spotted her from *Racundra*, while visiting Reval: '*Kittiwake* herself, unkempt, dilapidated, lovable little thing...'

There followed a fishing and sailing dinghy (no name recorded). Once arrived in Riga, according to the Autobiography 'A Lettish [i.e. Latvian] boat-builder made me, in a few days, a small boat for fishing and sailing with a fishbox built around the centreboard case and a small leg-of-mutton sail.'

Racundra, built 1921-22, brought together three elements: designer Otto Eggers, whom the Ransomes met, and 'fell in love with' a few days after acquiring *Kittiwake*; the Lettish builder of the dinghy, and Ransome's own vision of an ideal boat. 'Years of planning went into her before ever a line was drawn on paper,' as he wrote on the first page of *Racundra*'s first cruise.

Ransome wanted a boat 'that one man could manage if need be, but on which three could live comfortably.' He wanted a writing-table 'a full yard square', a place for a typewriter, broad bunks and full standing headroom. Eggers—'the best designer in the Baltic'—dutifully incorporated all this into his design. The result was something of a floating soapdish, enormously beamy, at nearly twelve feet (3.5m) on a length of just under thirty feet (9m). Her draught was three feet six inches with centreboard up, seven feet six inches with it lowered. Heavily-built, with a broad iron keel, a bluff bow and a rounded stern, she had more than a bit of Baltic trader and Colin Archer about her. Ketch-rigged, and without a bowsprit, she carried quite a modest 430 square feet of sail.

Ransome had written and published numerous books prior to this time, but *Racundra* was to give him the first (with the possible exception of *Old Peter's Russian Tales*) by which he would be remembered; certainly *Racundra's First Cruise* established at a stroke his reputation as a writer on sailing. The book, published in 1923, recounted the building, and launch (much delayed) and then his, Evgenia's and 'the Ancient's' first voyage in the August and September of 1922. 'The Ancient'—short for, obviously, The Ancient Mariner—was Carl Sehmel, wise, practical sailor, veteran of the tea-clipper *Thermopylae*, and in due course to be resurrected and immortalised as 'Peter Duck', in the book, and later the boat, of that name. He is in fact commemorated in *Racundra*'s own name, built up of *Ra*, for Ransome, *C* for Carl, *und*—the Latvian form of 'and'—and then *Ra* again for Evgenia, even though she was not yet officially Mrs Ransome.

They sailed from Riga on 20 August, going via Runo and the Moon Sound to Reval and Helsingfors in Finland, and back again on 26 September: just 38 days.

The second cruise, the following year, was compressed initially by the writing-up of the first, and interrupted by business trips to London and Moscow, gales and engine problems. They managed 24 days, including a visit to Helsinki and the Finnish archipelago which Ransome described as 'one of the pleasantest of our voyages.' But no book resulted.

In 1924, a short week-long delivery cruise, 15-23 May, Reval to Riga, preceded the third cruise. Partly written-up (as *Racundra Goes Inland*) and posthumously

Racundra (1921–5), Riga, Latvia

published (as *Racundra's Third Cruise*) in 2002, it saw her travel inland from Riga along the Aa (now Lieupe) river to Mitau (Jelgrava)—some 45 miles—and back. They started on 1 August and finished on 10 September—the longest time, if not distance, of their three annual cruises. In November, they returned to England to live and put *Racundra* up for sale.

The purchaser was K. Adlard Coles, a young yachting writer, who took her over in July 1925, planning to sail her back to England, and write a book about it, which he did. The book was *Close Hauled*, but the boat in it goes under the name of *Annette II*, as Ransome has made it a condition of the purchase that the name *Racundra* be not used.

Coles found *Racundra/Annette* 'a fine sea boat but in no way an ordinary vessel… She had many good points besides many faults: but she was not ordinary.'

His description of his first sight of her is very appreciative: '…she was quite unmistakable: bluff-bowed, beamy, strong-looking, with the fine pointed stern that I have often admired in Scandinavian ships. A ladder was brought and we climbed up to her deck. Here the beam of nearly twelve feet looked very conspicuous but not unpleasing; for the lines, guided by a good designer, were true.'

He is, inevitably, impressed by the cabin:

Cabin is perhaps not the right word; for the pride of *Annette* should rather be termed a room. It is huge for a twelve-ton yacht; it is even large for a twenty-ton yacht, being about ten feet long, about eight wide and full six high. It is possible to walk about, to stretch one's arms, to dress, to think without any restraint. On each side lie wide bunks, backed by ample lockers. A table occupies the centre, and in one corner is a desk large enough for a full-sized chart.

His summing-up in the book's Appendix is rather more critical, and perceptive of *Racundra*'s shortcomings.

This small sail area of 430 feet was in some ways a disadvantage, for it made her slow in normal weather. She took so long to make a passage that there was always a danger of getting caught out before making port. In fact to make five knots she required half a gale of wind, which, of course, piled up a large sea for so small a ship.

Close Hauled is in many ways a disappointing book. It is clear that Coles found pottering about the Baltic tedious and irksome, and this infects the writing—aptly summed-up in the choice of title. It only really takes off once they escape into the North Sea, and encounter a gale. Curiously, *Annette* made landfall in Southwold, which is where *Nancy Blackett* was lying when we bought her.

Racundra went through eight subsequent owners after Coles sold her in 1926. The last of these, Rod Pickering, found her in Morocco in 1976 and after carrying out some restoration sailed her across the Atlantic to Caracas, Venezuela. Around 1979, while being sailed single-handed by Pickering off the Venezuelan coast, *Racundra* hit a reef on La Rogues and was abandoned. It is assumed, though not proven, that she broke up there. Pickering continued to be registered as her owner up to and indeed beyond his disappearance at sea in 1982.

By 1928 the Ransomes had settled into Low Ludderburn; Arthur was writing for the *Manchester Guardian*, and they has renewed acquaintance with the Altounyan family, Ernest and Dora (née Collingwood, and one of Arthur's old flames) and their four children: Taqui, Susan, Titty and Roger, as well as the baby Brigit, born in 1926. In 1928 Arthur and Ernest decided to teach the four eldest to sail, and between them bought two second-hand lugsail dinghies, for £15 apiece.

Both were rather heavily-built boats more suited to estuary than lake sailing—perhaps the two grown-ups felt they would be safer. They were each about 14ft in length with clinker hulls.

Swallow, named by them after an old Collingwood family boat, had a six-inch-deep keel rather than a centreboard, an unusual arrangement for a sailing dinghy which could be accounted for by conversion from a rowing-boat. She was ballasted by pigs of lead, six of them with a combined weight of 100lb under the bottom-boards. She was painted white, with a deep, contrasting sheerstrake, and a brown sail. *Mavis* (Titty's real name) did have a centreboard, and was varnished, though later painted white. She was a little narrower in the beam than *Swallow*.

On Arthur Ransome's birthday in 1929, the Altounyan children presented him with a pair of red leather Turkish slippers. He was immensely touched, and

Swallow (1928–35): Ransome sailing her at Bowness on Windermere

Mavis (later *Amazon*), (1928–) seen here on Coniston, 1957, with Ernest Altounyan

this gift was the catalyst that triggered *Swallows and Amazons*. Clearly when the boats came to be put into a book, some changes had to be made—*Swallows and Mavises* is scarcely a stirring title.

When the Altounyans left for Syria a few days later, it was agreed that Ransome should have *Swallow*; *Mavis* remained in the Collingwood boathouse at Lanehead.

Eventually, in 1935, when the Ransomes had decided to move to the East Coast, *Swallow* was put up for sale. Her purchaser was a 15-year-old schoolboy, Roger Fothergill. In 1996, he wrote to me from his home in the British Virgin Islands to fill in what he could of *Swallow*'s subsequent career.

'I came to hear that a sailing dinghy was for sale at Walker's boatyard, just north of the Ferry Nab. On going to inspect her, I learned from 'Ernie' Walker, son of the locally famous 'Gentleman George' Walker, that she was being sold by a Mr Arthur Ransome and was called *Swallow*.

'This made me prick up my ears because I had read *Swallows and Amazons* and *Swallowdale*, still had them in fact. On seeing the little vessel all doubt was removed as she still had the ballast box in her bottom amidships which was something of a unique feature.'

He traded in a canoe for her, and 'became the proud owner for the equivalent of £14.'

Although the young Roger was familiar with the books, he was not in awe of the boat and set about modifying her to his liking. 'She came to me exactly as described in Ransome's books, being rigged with a standing lug mainsail and nothing else. But I soon found that she carried enough weather helm as to be improved in balance with the addition of a jib, and this I had installed; it was tacked down to a short iron bumkin which projected beyond her bow about 9in.

'The other alteration which I made was to have the lead pigs of ballast, which she carried in a special box, cast into a single piece and secured to a ballast keel which I caused to be made, about one foot deep at the stern, rising to 6in near to the bow. She made very much less leeway afterwards.'

Roger added, unapologetically: 'If you accuse me of vandalism, or even desecration, I fear I am guilty as charged; all I can say in my defence is that I know my job too, and greatly improved her performance.'

He kept *Swallow* for several years, not only on Windermere—he paints a lovely picture of the little boat reaching out into the sort of waters imagined in *Peter
Duck*. 'My horizons were expanding and I longed to get to the salt water. The lake
was altogether too confining, and though incomparably more beautiful than the
tidal flats of the Kent estuary at the head of Morecambe Bay, where I finally based
her, the latter place had one overriding advantage over the lake—simply that the
muddy water that swirled around my boat when the flood made, was exactly the
same sheet of water that broke into thundering confusion on the coral reefs of the
Pacific atolls or that laved the golden beaches of the Carribean Cays. All that was
needed was the courage to set out.'

It's worth pausing here to reflect that this same restlessness, this longing to
set sail on tidal waters evidently infected Ransome himself, at about the same
time. It surfaces first in the imaginary adventure of *Peter Duck*, and soon after in
reality, with the decision to move to the East Coast and the purchase of *Nancy
Blackett*.

But back to Roger Fothergill, and *Swallow*. Needless to say, he didn't reach
those distant shores, not at least in *Swallow*, but 'whenever enough water, daylight and a convenient wind all occurred at the same time, I cruised to Grange-
over-Sands, Flookborough, Sandside, Silverdale and once even distant (to me)
Morecambe itself. Sleeping under the awning, spread over the boom, and cooking
on a Primus stove—heaven!'

Eventually when work—apprenticed to a shipping line—intervened, he laid
Swallow up at Crosfields, the boatbuilders at Arnside. Incidentally, in another letter, to Stuart Weir, he cast doubt on the popular belief that Crosfields built *Swallow*: 'I had known Fred Crosfield all my short life and if they had built her Fred
would certainly have recognized her and told me so. But they looked after her for
two years and he never mentioned it.' Not long before the war broke out in 1939,
he asked Fred Crosfield to sell her for him. After that he lost sight of her, though
he imagined that Fred would have sold her to someone local.

Mavis remained with the Altounyan family and was still owned by them in
the 1980s. She was kept in the boathouse at Nibthwaite, at the bottom end of
Coniston, and regularly sailed by Roger. On one occasion she disappeared from
the boathouse and was discovered tied up to a tree not far away. She was brought

home, and Roger put a notice on her: 'This is a very old boat in peaceful retirement. Please do not disturb her.'

Roger died in 1987, and the family decided to hand over *Mavis* to the Windermere Steamboat Museum. Back in 1958, Ernest Altounyan had painstakingly sheathed *Mavis* in glassfibre to preserve her timbers, but once at the museum it was quickly found that this was exactly what was not happening. The glassfiibre was stripped off, and the hull was found to need extensive restoration. It was at this point that Christina Hardyment launched her appeal to raise £5,000 for the work. The appeal, which was successful, led directly to the formation of the Arthur Ransome Society.

Its inaugural meeting, at the Steamboat museum, was marked by the ceremony to rename *Mavis* (not exactly a relaunch—the restoration, which has proved more complex than anticipated, was not quite completed). Henceforth she would, officially so to speak, carry the name by which millions of readers already recognised her: *Amazon*. The name was spoken by the original 'ship's baby', Brigit Sanders (nee Altounyan), who became TARS' first president. And the child chosen to smash the bottle of grog over *Amazon*'s bows was none other than Katy Jennings, the Scarborough girl who, just a year previously, had persuaded her father to drive her down to Suffolk to see *Nancy Blackett*, having written to Mike Rines begging to be included on her first voyage to Holland.

In *Amazon*'s early years at the Steamboat Museum, it was sometimes possible to take her for a sail, if the wind wasn't too strong. Now, though, she has slipped further into 'peaceful retirement' and is allowed out only for the occasional row.

In 2007 the Steamboat Museum closed for refurbishment of itself and its exhibits, following their acqustion by the Lakeland Arts Trust, on behalf of the nation in lieu of tax. *Amazon* was not included in this transfer, and has been moved, perhaps temporarily, to the Ruskin Museum at Coniston.

Coch-y-bonddhu, also restored, is a less well-known Ransome dinghy, though she too has a literary role—she appears in *The Picts and the Martyrs* as *Scarab*, the new dinghy built for Dick and Dot. And Ransome kept her far longer than any of his other boats—twenty years.

A thirteen-foot clinker-built lugsail dingy, she was built in 1934 by Crosfields of Arnside, who had also built *Swallow*, initially for Ransome's fishing friend Charles Renold, hence her name, *Coch-y-bonddhu*, after a fishing fly (and a mix of Welsh and Gaelic). Ransome was, ostensibly, trying to develop his friend's interest in sailing; however, Ransome's own intense interest in the dinghy's build suggests otherwise. He kept a close eye on it, and reported by letter to Renold: 'She is all but finished planking and we have to report that you are in very great luck. How the devil they do it, I do not know, but they have got hold of the most beautiful spruce for the planking and a really lovely bit of wood for the keel and stem and covering board. I think you have got a real bargain in her and we are both full of envy.'

Renolds tried the dinghy, but he did not really take to sailing and soon made the boat over to Ransome. When the Ransomes moved to East Anglia in 1935, '*Cocky*' went with them. Much lighter in build than *Swallow*, and equipped with a centreboard, she seemed ideal for sailing from the Ransomes' riverside home at Levington, and acting as a tender to the newly-acquired *Nancy Blackett*. She soon proved too heavy for that role; a pram dinghy called *Queen Mary* (see below) was built for the job. But *Cocky* continued to provide Ransome with dinghy sailing, and a quick way of getting from his home to *Nancy*'s Pin Mill mooring on the other side of the Orwell river. He would also tow *Cocky* round to the Walton Backwaters, and go sailing in her when he was supposed to be working aboard *Nancy*.

It was one afternoon when he was hauling *Cocky* ashore at Levington Creek that he met the young Josephine and George Russell, newly moved-in to nearby Broke Hall. The children regularly crewed on *Nancy*, and later *Selina King*, and at one stage Ransome lent them *Cocky* for a while.

When the Ransomes returned to the lakes in 1940, *Cocky* accompanied them and their new home, the Heald, on the eastern shore of Coniston Water, provided her with a convenient private harbour from which her owner could take her out to sail and fish.

After the war, in 1945, the Ransomes moved to London, leaving *Cocky* laid-up until 1948 when they returned, buying Lowick Hall, before moving south again, this time for good, in 1950. *Cocky* was again laid up, and eventually sold in 1954.

She went to Earnseat School at Arnside, where she was used for sailing les-

Coch-y-bonddhu (1934–54), seen here on the Walton Backwaters

sons. The headmaster's son, Edward Barnes, also sailed—and maintained—her, as he told us when he visited *Cocky* on one of her reunions with *Nancy* in the 1990s. Ths school called her *Swallow*, possibly in the belief that she was in fact the original *Swallow*. Eventually she was sold by the school, taken to Scotland and lost track of.

It was not until 1991 that the trail picked up again. A newspaper report on the formation of the Scottish branch of the Arthur Ransome Society led to a phone call to its convenor, Dr Christopher Birt, from one Jeff Parker-Eaton who had bought *Cocky* from the school, at which he worked, in 1968 and subsequently moved to the West Coast of Scotland, taking her with him. He had later sold her to Hendersons boatyard in Mallaig who had sold her on to the Kilcamb Lodge Hotel at Strontian, where Chris Birt eventually found her, lying upside down on the lawn. She had not been used for many years and was in poor condition, thought the spars and sails, having been stored under cover, had fared much better.

Chris and the hotel's new owner Gordon Blakeway agreed to work together to restore her. She was gifted by the Blakeways to the Arthur Ransome Society who moved her into expert care, and launched an appeal to raise funds for her restoration. This raised the needed £4500 and the work was undertaken by John Hodgson of Fiunary in Morven, who by happy coincidence had served his apprenticeship at Crosfields.

Cocky was relaunched in 1995, appropriately by Josephine Russell, and appropriately at the Kilcamb Lodge. She has subsequently been actively sailed, both in the Lake District and on the East Coast, in care of the Nancy Blackett Trust. When not in use she was on display at the Windermere Steamboat Museum until its 2007 closure. In 2008 she travelled to Falmouth to form part of the *Swallows and Amazons* exhibition at the National Maritime Museum Cornwall. She is currently kept, ashore and under cover, at Windermere School.

Queen Mary, a small pram dinghy, was built for *Nancy Blackett* in 1936 after *Coch-y-bonddhu* proved too heavy to act as a tender. She was built in Bembridge, Isle of Wight, on the advice of Herbert Hanson, and delivered by rail (plus ferry and road) to Pin Mill.

Selina King, built as the successor to *Nancy Blackett*, was undoubtedly the finest yacht Ransome owned, a sleek, fast, canoe-sterned thirty-five-footer. He went to a renowned designer, Fred Shepherd for her and she was one of two yachts built for Ransome by Kings at Pin Mill. The motivation for her build, and the decision to sell *Nancy Blackett,* was Evgenia's dissatisfaction with the space aboard *Nancy*, particularly in her galley. Ransome conceived and sketched the design while in hospital recovering from an umbilical hernia.

Selina was launched with suitable ceremony on 28 September 1938. Ransome got very little sailing out of the residue of that year, and although the summer of 1939 yielded some enjoyable local sailing, it was overshadowed by the impending war, and in due course *Selina* had to be laid up. Ransome chose to take her to Oulton Broad, and set sail on 26 September. He was forced to take refuge in Southwold, 'that horrible harbour', and was then kept gale-bound there the next day. Thus it was that on 28 September, the first anniversary of *Selina*'s launch, Ransome sailed her for what was to be the last time into Lowestoft, to be laid up for the duration of the war. By the time it was over, six years later, his health had deteriorated and he was forbidden by his doctors to sail *Selina*. She had to be sold.

In March, 1946 she was sold, for £1,600, £200 less than the asking price and some £900 less than the value put on her by Ransome's broker. The buyer was Peter Davies, the publisher of yachting books, and the first of several owners through whom she eventually moved to the south coast.

The most significant figure in her post-Ransome history however proved to be a taxi driver in Bermuda. 'Captain' Hal White also ran yacht charters and was saving money to buy his own boat. Eventually some regular clients, an American couple, offered to lend him the money to go ahead. He started scanning yachting magazines and quickly discovered, and immediately fell in love with, *Selina King*, then owned by Commander Blewett. Hal bought her in 1963, for £3,500, and arranged for a delivery crew to sail her back to Bermuda—he had to fly back to earn the money to pay them.

Hal chartered her happily for nine years (guests included Ted Kennedy) before deciding he needed a bigger boat. Twenty-five years later, in 1997, when he was thinking about downscaling, his bride Ruth suggested what he wanted was *Selina*. 'That's all I needed—the Jack was out of the box.' He had kept in touch

Selina King (1938–46), at Pin Mill with *Swallow II* in tow

Peter Duck (1946–49) at Pin Mill

with *Selina* for a while after he sold her, but latterly had lost track of her. He eventually tracked her down to Coconut Grove, Florida, where she proved to be in a distressing, dilapidated condition. Mastless, rotten, paint peeling, seams opening, she had been untouched for several seasons and was being kept afloat by a solar panel and a pump.

'She really was a mess,' according to Hal, 'She was barely breathing.' She had in fact just been sold, but Hal, strengthened by the opinion of a boatbuilding acquaintance—'she's a powerful little vessel, she's well put together and she's got a lot of life in her'—persuaded the new owner that he, Hal, was the one to restore her.

So he did, and sailed her out of Hamilton Harbour, Bermuda until the mid-2000s when he decided the time really had come to swallow the anchor. He contacted me in 2007 to see if the NBT would be interested in acquiring her. We were, but the difficulties of bringing her across the Atlantic, and the open-ended nature of the costs of putting her into the condition needed to earn her keep chartering in the UK, and the inevitable distraction from our first responsibility of taking care of *Nancy,* militated against the proposal and eventually we had to walk away from it, with great regret. In 2008, we heard that Hal had succeeded in finding a buyer for *Selina.* Later that same year he was diagnosed with a brain tumour, and passed away on 5 March 2009.

Selina's new owner, a Canadian called Michael ('Monty') Lamontagne, planned to keep her in Bermuda initially, but in a few years' time to take her through the Panama Canal and up the west coast of America to Vancouver Island. Alas, this was a dream destined to remain unfulfilled – the work needed on *Selina* proved too much for the relatively inexperienced young shipwright and in 2011 I had a phone call from her new owner, Martin Pollard, who had a business in Bermuda but also kept up a home in England and planned eventually to return her to the UK. Martin has pressed ahead with what proved to be an extensive restoration. In August 2017, *Selina* was unloaded from a a yacht transporter ship at Southampton Docks and moved to a shed in West Sussex where her restoration was to be completed, with the hope that she will be relaunched in time for her 80th birthday in 2018.

Swallow (2), built 1938 by Kings of Pin Mill as tender to *Selina King,* and completed alongside her, was a ten-foot clinker dinghy. She also served with *Peter Duck*, before being sold in the early 1950s to the Imber family. It was on their lawn, upsided down, that she was discovered by Roger Wardale in 1989, following a phone call from Brigit Sanders who had been tipped-off by a friend of the Imbers. Roger was to be a founder TARS member and both national and Southern regional chairman; he has written various books on Ransome, notably *Arthur Ransome Under Sail*, (first published in 1991 as *Nancy Blackett: Under Sail with Arthur Ransome*). Once he had confirmed her identity, and the Imbers had donated her, Roger took her restoration in hand, assisted by some of the 11-year-olds from the school at which he taught. This *Swallow* has since participated in numerous TARS events and in 2008 joined *Coch-y-bonddhu* at the Falmouth maritime museum exhibition where, despite being correctly labelled, she no doubt misled less attentive visitors into thinking they were viewing the 'real thing'.

If *Selina King* was the classiest of Ransome's boats, then *Peter Duck* could claim to have proved the most successful of the three that he had specially designed for himself (the others being *Selina* herself and *Racundra*). Not that he thought so at the time. He found fault with the design, commissioned from J. Laurent Giles, during the building (again, by King's of Pin Mill), after cracking his head on a beam above his bunk that was six inches lower than he had been anticipating. Neither was he best pleased with Giles' presumption in naming the craft after Ransome's character Peter Duck—though the name did stick. As soon as she was built, in October 1946, but before she was rigged he sold her to Giles and his partner Humphrey Barton for the cost of building, £1,200, but relented after a month, and bought her back, for £300 more than he had received for her. Once she had been rigged, 1947 yielded a fair amount of sailing, encompassing much pleasure including the discovery of West Mersea, but Ransome did not sail her at all in 1948, moving back to the Lake District in the summer, and, according to his log, made only one short trip in 1949, before selling her.

The cause of Ransome's dissatisfaction with *Peter Duck* is perhaps revealed in the brief he gave to Laurent Giles: 'A marine bath-chair for my old age'—a far cry from the racy and elegant *Selina* which his advancing years and deteriorating health had forced him to give up.

Nevertheless, Giles had come up with a practical and manageable boat, combining easily-handled ketch rig with a flat underwater profile giving shallow draught, and a 'rather motor-boaty bow' in keeping with her proposed status as a 50/50 motorsailer. A beefier engine than the installed 8hp Stuart Turner might have been more in keeping with this brief, and in due course, it was replaced.

It was in 1957, after two intervening owners, that *Peter Duck* came into the hands of the family that—like Ransome—owned her twice, but—unlike him—has kept and cherished her, for over forty of her sixty-odd years. George Jones was a yacht broker, based at Waldringfield on the River Deben, trading as the East Coast Yacht Agency. He was also something of an artist (his brother was yacht designer J. Francis Jones) and secretary of the barge preservation group the East Coast Sail Trust (owners of the Thames barge *Thalatta*).

George and his wife June saw their children grow up aboard and around *Peter Duck* and he liked the design so much that in 1960 he launched a slightly-modified version as the 'Peter Duck' class. Laurent Giles added an extra plank to the hull, to increase headroom (which Ransome would no doubt have approved of) and extended the coachroof forward of the main mast, now mounted on its top in a tabernacle. The class design is three inches longer with four inches more draught than the original *Peter Duck*. Solidly built of iroko on oak frames by Porter and Haylett of Wroxham, the class filled a niche in postwar yachting needs, and between 1960 and 1970 thirty-eight were built, most still sailing.

The family kept *Peter Duck* until 1984. In 1988, she was bought by Greg and Ann Palmer, Ransome fans who sailed her far and wide, including round England and the part of Scotland that is south of the Caledonian Canal. Eventually, in 1994 they sailed to St Petersburg to help visionary boatbuilder Vladimir Martous with his project to build a replica of Peter the Great's flagship the *Shtandart*. Sadly, Greg died there following a stroke in 1997.

The following year, Ann arranged for *Peter Duck* to be sailed back to the UK, skippered by John Robinson (of Heritage Afloat fame) with a young Russian crew. They had to pump all the way, because the Russian winters had taken their toll below the waterline and she leaked badly. She made it back in time to take part in the Portsmouth International Festival of the Sea that year, and a few weeks later, George Jones' daughter Julia received a phone call from a friend in Woodbridge:

'*Peter Duck* came up the river last night. She's in the Ferry Dock now—and up for sale.' Early the following morning, Julia, her partner the writer and journalist Francis Wheen and her brother Ned were on the quay. 'We were hardly able to contain our emotion at seeing her again, so familiar, so weathered and with the courtesy flags of seven nations in her locker.'

She was a bit more than weathered. Ice had penetrated her planking. There was rot, cracked timbers and other horrors. When they unshipped her rudder it fell into three pieces. By a mixture of rather sweet coincidences it was Karl Marx—he who had inspired the Russian Revolution through which Ransom had made his name as a journalist—who saved the day. Francis, like Ransome a Guardian journalist, was finishing a biography of Marx. The royalties from it went into saving *Peter Duck*, as the name of her tender now commemorates. In June 1999, a delighted crowd of wellwishers gathered on the narrow quay outside Frank Knight's workshop at Woodbridge to see a revitalised *Peter Duck* swung out and lowered gently into the water.

Since then, the 'dear old Duck' as Julia likes to call her, has settled naturally back into the role of a family boat, for a third generation of Joneses, her sturdy, duck-egg green hull becoming a familiar sight on the Deben and adjacent rivers, and finding time to engage with local Arthur Ransome Society events and maritime festivals. Julia herself has emerged as an impressive children's novelist, Ransome-inspired but with a keen ear for the themes and preoccupations of the twenty-first century. Her books are set on the River Orwell and the wider East Coast, on a variety of boats and with sailing and seamanship at their heart.

By 1951 the Ransomes were living, somewhat improbably, in London's suburbs, in a flat overlooking the Thames at Hurlingham Court, Putney. The idea of owning a boat once again appealed, this time as an annexe they could escape to in the summer. Sooner or later they gravitated to Hillyards' Littlehampton yard, where they saw a twenty-seven-foot canoe-sterned five-and-a-half-tonner with a centre cockpit which they liked. At the London Motor Show that autumn they saw a part-built version, and before the end of the show had signed the contract. They promptly registered her name: *Lottie Blossom*, after a character in P. G. Wodehouse's novel *The Luck of the Bodkins* (she's a film star who keeps an alligator in her laundry basket to deter customs officers from searching it).

They took delivery—on time for once, to Ransome's amazement—at the end of March, 1952, but did not sail her round to Chichester Harbour until mid-April, eventually settling into Birdham Pool. Ill-health prevented further sailing until the very end of June. Trials within Chichester Harbour convinced Ransome that '*Lottie* can sail, and sail very well. In fact she is not a 50/50 boat but a 75/75. We thought her 75% motor boat on coming round from Littlehampton and after yesterday's good sail thought her at least 75% sailing boat.' (Log, 17 July).

While sailing in the harbour they came across a couple of old friends, both as it happened in Bosham Creek: *Peter Duck* on 29 July, 'now blue', and a month or so later, 26 August 'a man called Cook' took the Ransomes to see *Racundra*, 'lying in the mud, looking much the same, a very good, intelligent hull, but she now has some sort of silly doghouse, and, of course, an earlier owner had cut the great beam that carried the bridge deck.' In both cases, Ransome records 'Genia would not look at her,' but of *Racundra* he adds 'I would have liked to know just what has been done to her.'

This, though was after their first long sea-voyage to Buckler's Hard, which was to become a favourite destination, via Bursledon on the Hamble on the way out, where they stayed for the best part of a week, and Yarmouth ('charming little town in itself, but a perfect hell as a harbour on an August weekend') on the return trip.

It was to be their only long cruise of the season, and indeed in this *Lottie*. By 8 September they were 'talking of *Lottie Minor* [public-school speak for younger sibling] with identical hull, but tiller steering, and a real single-hander, which *Lottie B* can never be.' To be fair, the centre-cockpit *Lottie* can be and has been singe-handed, and Ransome's dream of single-handing her successor was never realised. The problem with the Mark I version was more likely to do with an incident in which Ransome lowered the mainsail and enveloped Genia, in the centre cockpit, in it. By October, they were back at the Motor Show, talking details of the new boat with David Hillyard.

Centre-cockpit *Lottie* quickly found a buyer in Sir Paul Mallinson, who in accordance with Ransome's insistence on retaining the *Lottie Blossom* name for his new boat, renamed her *Ragged Robin III*. Under this name she went on to have a number of owners, including Anthony Rushworth-Lund who wrote an engaging minor classic *By Way of the Golden Isles* about cruising her to the Mediterranean, and Peter St John Howe, who clocked up 1,000 miles single-handed in 1991-92.

She is now in the capable hands of Ted and Diana Evans, both Ransome fans, who keep her moored just below their flat in the Granary at Woodbridge.

The second, aft-cockpit, tiller-steered, *Lottie*, was otherwise, apart from the single cabin, similar to the first version, five and a half tons with canoe stern. Ransome, as his log shows, took an active interest in her in the first quarter of 1953, but this did not prevent her overrunning her planned launch date of 1 April. On 3 May they took her round to Chichester Harbour, and on 10 May they set off for Buckler's Hard, this time via Bursledon and Yarmouth (where the harbourmaster was the same one who had been there during *Nancy*'s gale-bound stay of September 1935).

They returned to Itchenor on 18 May, but on the 25th they were off to Buckler's Hard again, basing themselves there, with sails to Lymington and Spithead to examine the ships assembled for the Fleet Review. Eventually, on 26 June, they left Buckler's Hard for Cherbourg. They enjoyed Cherbourg very much and socialised with fellow RCC boats, before returning overnight on 5/6 July. A long, sociable layover at Bursledon was followed by a short sociable visit to Buckler's Hard before returning to Itchenor. Another visit to Buckler's Hard was fitted in before lay-up in Littlehampton at the end of the season.

The following season, 1954, the Ransomes set out for Chichester on 11 May, but met a head wind and turned back. The following day they started out again, but outside Chichester Harbour yielded to temptation and carried on to Buckler's Hard instead. They saw some aeroplanes towing targets to be fired at from the shore—'a row of heavy splashes close by suggested that we should do well not to linger'—and later, 'a thundering seaplane passed by heading N.'

They picked up a mooring and the following day lunched at the *Master Builder's* where they learnt that 'good old Watty Snooks the driver and man we liked so much' had died following a car accident, and had been buried that same day. 'The village gave him a very affectionate send off. Everybody liked him and one of the

The first *Lottie Blossom* (1952), now *Ragged Robin III*

The second *Lottie Blossom* (1953–4), Chichester Harbour

pleasures of coming to Buckler's Hard was the gossipy drive with him to the station.' They made an attempt to get away the following day, but turned back, and were rewarded by hearing a 'pleasant story of George V over the naming of the *Queen Mary*. The builders had called her the *Queen Victoria* among themselves but had waited before making an official announcement. George went to see her and asked one of the foremen what was to be her name. The foreman replied, 'Well, your Majesty, we thought of naming her after one of England's greatest queens!' 'Oh, she will be pleased!' said George, beaming, and they knew she was the *Queen Mary*, and announced the name at once.'

On the 17th, in the Master Builder's, they were introduced to fellow RCC member George Millar (author, as Ransome notes, of *A White Boat from England*, published recently, and a number of other excellent books), but Ransome failed to realise who he was.

This was the first of three visits during the season. On the second trip, they saw a Dutch liner apparently grounding on the Bramble Bank. 'We felt *Lottie* not powerful enough to help.' This time, they stayed for the whole of the month of June, apart from a visit to London for Ransome to see his doctor for a check-up, and left at the end of the month for Cherbourg. The log tells of a succession of incidents involving fouled moorings and incompetent crews interspersed with the odd good meal and convivial encounter, rounded off with a succession of lows ('perturbations' as the French met office calls them') preventing departure. They got back to Itchenor on 20 July and within days, 'By train from London to Littlehampton for the day where saw Hillyard and told him we were giving up & would sell the boat.'

Nevertheless they carried on for the remainder of the season, and spent much time trying to track down recurrent problems with the engine. Both Hillyards and the maker, Stuart Turner (!) recommended an engineer called Noyce in Itchenor who came out and identified a number of problems, including the dynamo which was running much too fast (it later proved to have been set up to run at double or treble the correct speed). In early August they went to Buckler's Hard, where they visited *Peter Duck* ('The owners do not try to use the bunks in the cabin.') but cut short the visit and returned to Itchenor after a phone-call to Noyce who wanted to try a passage on *Lottie*. The engine behaved well while he was aboard. Twelve days later (17 August) they made passage again to Buckler's Hard, the engine behaving temperamentally, as it did on the return passage on the 20th, finally conking out at the entrance to Chichester Harbour, with *Lottie* being carried up by the tide, with little steerage way. This resulted in Evgenia tearing her hand badly in trying to pick up a buoy under sail, and Ransome catching a fingernail. A doctor was found, who bound up Genia's hand—she had feared she might lose the use of it—and also dressed Ransome's finger 'cheerfully remarking that I might lose the nail.'

On the 22nd Ransome records sailing with Penman in *Duette* and John Mac-Namara in *Beltane*. On the 23rd, with 'only two good hands between us,' they ship a crewman, Bob, and make their last passage, back to Littlehampton. They find a good breeze, and twice have to heave to being ahead of the tide. 'A really delightful passage,' as Ransome described it in a letter to his friend Busk... 'It was a grand sail yesterday, fresh fair wind, exactly of the strength *Lottie* best likes... easily the best sail of the year.' On 30 August the log concludes with the brief and businesslike entry: 'Mast out and into shed.'

And that was it; the end of a sailing career that spanned over 30 years. *Lottie* went through another eleven owners until Roger Wardale, with the help of another TARS member, Paul Crisp, tracked her down in a garden near Guildford in Surrey in 1990. Her owner, Christopher Barlow, had had her since 1983 and was at that time engaged in an extensive, and slow, restoration on the boat. But, despite being one of the 'three skippers,' along with Mike Rines of *Nancy Blackett* and Greg Palmer of *Peter Duck*, to whom Wardale's book '*Nancy Blackett: Under Sail with Arthur Ransome*' was dedicated, he moved house without leaving any forwarding address, and both he and *Lottie* have vanished without trace. Her whereabouts are a mystery, though the assumption that the restoration started going backwards, as so many do, and that *Lottie* is no more, remains regrettably the most likely explanation.

'Which ship is flagship?' demands Captain John after the sea-battle in *Swallows and Amazons*. Captain Nancy unhesitatingly replies '*Swallow*'. But which ship deserves to be considered the flagship of Ransome's serial fleet of yachts and boats? Is *Nancy Blackett* truly 'the best little boat I ever had'? She is after all only a run-of-the-mill production model Hillyard. *Selina King*, her successor, was larger and finer, and custom-designed for Ransome by a highly respected designer. *Racundra*, too, was custom-built, with many of Ransome's own ideas incorporated, as indeed was *Peter Duck*. (Both the *Lottie*s, though built for Ransome, were off-the-shelf Hillyard designs.) But then, as Ransome himself said, 'Fools build and wise men buy.'

And in terms of sheer sailing miles, *Nancy* is the clear winner. Ransome sailed her much more than any of his other boats—about 1,600 nautical miles over the three and a bit seasons he owned her, between 1935 and 1938. *Racundra* managed only just over 1,000 miles over her three seasons, 1922-24, a very similar mileage to the second *Lottie Blossom*, thirty years later. Of the others, *Selina* managed around 450 miles in one intense season, 1939, in addition to the fifty Ransome squeezed in after he took delivery of her in late 1938—it's fair to say that had the war not intervened he would have got a great deal more sailing out of her. *Peter Duck* managed 300 miles in 1947-49 (though none at all in '48), and the first *Lottie* sailed 200 miles in 1951, before being sold to make way for her successor.

Selina may have given him the prestige, and no doubt the thrilling sailing, that befitted the noted author he had become (and the galley that met the demands of the noted author's wife), but it was, after all, *Nancy* that helped him to gain the literary reputation, and indeed the income to pay for *Selina*.

Racundra, too, produced a book, and one in which she appears under her own name. It would be a brave or foolish commentator who tried to weigh the respective merits of *Racundra's First Cruise* and *We Didn't Mean to Go to Sea*—so here goes. I have to nail my colours firmly to *Nancy*'s mast on this issue, simply because while *Racundra's First Cruise* was also Ransome's first sailing book, it is simply a yarn about a sailing cruise, one among many, and we could argue enjoyably all night about which such books it is better than, or are better than it. Whereas, as I've hoped to show in earlier chapters, *We Didn't Mean to Go to Sea* is something unique—rich, condensed, full of references, a rite-of-passage novel that brings alive the joy and surprise of putting to sea for the first time, and making landfall in a distant, unknown place.

Acknowledgements

First and foremost to Mike Rines for his courageous and determined – and wildly over-budget – rescue and restoration of *Nancy Blackett*. Without him, she, and we, would not be here. Also for his assistance with archives, photographs, recollections, facts and general support.

Then to the late Roger Wardale, whose account of Mike's work along with his burrowings in the Brotherton Library's Special Collections section in his 1991 book *Nancy Blackett: Under Sail with Arthur Ransome* inspired me to launch the appeal and, to an extent, to produce this present book.

Also to Terry Absalom, my original 'partner in crime' who popped up out of nowhere soon after the appeal was launched, and put his shoulder to the wheel. Without his wealth of practical experience, initiative and good humour the Nancy Blackett Trust would not have become what it is. I doubt I'd have been capable of getting the show on the road—at least as quickly and effectively as we did—on my own. Terry died in 2006 after a long and typically courageous struggle with motor neurone disease. I still miss him.

The Nancy Blackett Trust has of course benefitted from the enthusiasm, skills and hard work of many other people as trustees, skippers, mates and just helpful and generous members, all of them volunteers. Some are mentioned in the text, but if I begin listing names here I simply won't know where to stop. So thank you to every member, and there are at least a thousand of you, past and present, for helping to keep *Nancy* afloat.

In putting this book together, my thanks are also due to the various other organisations surrounding the Ransome legacy. To the Red Slipper Fund of the Arthur Ransome Society for financial assistance. To the trustees of the Arthur Ransome Literary Estate, Geraint Lewis, Christina Hardyment and Paul Flint, for the use of Ransome's writings, photographs and drawings. Extracts from *We Didn't Mean to Go to Sea* by Arthur Ransome published by Jonathan Cape are reprinted by permission of the Random House Group, © Arthur Ransome 1940.

I'm also grateful to the Cruising Association for their kind co-operation regarding the use of Ransome's 'Saturday to Saturday' which first appeared in the CA *Bulletin*, 1937. This article has been reprinted several times, but only for private circulation, not — until now — for general publication.

Photographs: I'm grateful to Special Collections, Leeds University Library, where the Ransome archive is held, for permission to use the photos on pages 2, 42 and 206 (top) by Josephine Russell, and for those on p.p. 16, 192 and 213 (bottom), sources unknown. Other historic and restoration photos are from Mike Rines' collection. The photo on p. 49 is thanks to Alex Haig; on p. 116 by Elizabeth Ikin is courtesy of Charles Mapleston/Malachite Films; the wonderful *Mavis* photo on p. 198 is courtesy of Jonathan Lewis (who was aboard at the time); on p. 213 top is by Bill Wallace King.

In the colour section, plate 1 is by Suzanne Sheard; 2a from Mike Rines; 2b and 3a by Martin Lewis; 5 by Roger Sturge; 7b by Bill Wallace King. Others are my own. I'm also particularly grateful to John Perryman for the beautifully executed Lines of *Nancy Blackett*, which appear on p51.

Finally, thanks to the ever-wonderful Libby Purves for her Foreword, and to Claudia Myatt for the front cover illustration and the map on p.p. 46–7, and for her many other artistic contributions to the Nancy Blackett Trust.